Advance Praise for The Personal Branding Phenomenon

"This is wonderful: full of practical, important strategies for dramatically increasing your personal power and influence."

Brian Tracy
President
Brian Tracy International

"'If I only knew then, what I know now...' Peter has created the guide to help you avoid the frustration of this 'wisdom curve'! *The Personal Branding Phenomenon* will help everyone manage their careers, talents and lives for maximum impact and success."

Colin Mackenzie
Senior Vice President–Financial Advisor Division
Financial Network Investment Corporation

"Creating a truly successful brand, one that instantly puts your name in the minds of consumers and prospects everywhere, is the Holy Grail of marketing. I was skeptical when I first heard of Montoya's book, but after reading it, I've become a believer, and a practitioner of, *The Personal Branding Phenomenon*. Read it and see your brand come alive."

Karen Morstad
Vice President, Marketing
Royal Alliance Associates, Inc.

The
Personal Branding
Phenomenon

Realize greater influence, explosive income growth and rapid career advancement by applying the branding techniques of Michael, Martha & Oprah.

Peter Montoya

& Tim Vandehey

Contributions made by Paul Viti

PERSONAL
BRANDING
PRESS

FIRST EDITION PUBLISHED 2002

Second Printing 2002

1 2 3 4 5 6 7 8 9 0   DOC/DOC   0 9 8 7 6 5 4 3 2 1

ISBN 0-9674506-1-6   Price: $24.95

Library of Congress Catalog Card Number: 2002090498

Montoya, Peter.
    The personal branding phenomenon : realize greater
influence, explosive income growth and rapid career
advancement by applying the branding techniques of
Michael, Martha & Oprah / Peter Montoya & Tim Vandehey ;
contributions made by Paul Viti. -- 1st ed.
    p. cm.
    Includes index.
    LCCN 2002090498
    ISBN 0-9674506-1-6

    1. Brand name products--Marketing. 2. Success in
business.   I. Vandehey, Tim.   II. Title.

HD69.B7M66 2002   658.8'27
                             QBI02-200261

Personal Branding Press Publishing

This publication is designed to provide accurate and authoritative information in regard to the subject matter covered. It is sold with the understanding that the publisher is not engaged in rendering legal, accounting, or other professional services. If the legal advice or other expert assistance is required, the services of a competent professional person should be sought.

— From a declaration of principles jointly adopted by a committee of the American Bar Association and a committee of publishers.

Printed and bound by Vaughan Printing

Peter Montoya's books are available at special quantity discounts to use as premiums and sales promotions, or for use in corporate training programs. For more information, please contact us at www.petermontoya.com. or (866) 288-9300

Book Designed by Andrew Rea
Author Photography by Robert Randall

To the greatest Personal Brand I've ever known,
Louise "Grandcracker" Bowers

Table of Contents

Foreword

It's not always easy to see a revolution coming. When I saw the rough drafts of Peter Montoya's new book in the summer of 2001, I was impressed. He had grasped something that most of the so-called "gurus" of branding had not: that Personal Branding isn't just a tool for entrepreneurs and independent professionals. It can have powerful benefits for a corporate employee who wants to remain and excel within his or her company environment.

Peter's second insight was that the building of Personal Brands by employees is not a threat to the corporation, but an asset. That wasn't an easy sell for me; I've spent many years working for huge corporations, and I know the innate desire for control and the fear of independence, and of losing good people to the world of self-employment. The notion that corporate executives would be thrilled about 5,000 self-promoters working on the company dime to propagate their unique identity was a little hard to swallow.

Then I talked to Peter and gave the whole idea another think. I realized that Personal Branding in the corporate environment isn't about jockeying for promotions, but about a clearer definition of everyone's strengths and talents. In any large company, management often doesn't have a clear idea of the capabilities of about 80% of it's people. There are just too many people, too much work to do, and no clear way to separate hype from fact. So when a company is looking for leaders or experts, it's often a crapshoot.

Personal Branding is the remedy. Encouraged by management and passed down to the white-collar rank and file, its principles can help workers define their goals, identify their strengths, hone leadership qualities, and establish influence with co-workers in areas where they have the greatest experience or knowledge. This is the kind of environment where leaders spontaneously appear, where people are motivated to improve their skills, because the route to greater advancement is very clear.

I warned Peter about the possible downside: a workplace where everyone was worrying about their own Personal Brand and not about the company, thereby dragging everyone down. He acknowledged that was a risk, but told me that as long as executives and human resources personnel managed the culture change properly, people would continue to see their success within the framework of the corporation. Sure, you'd inevitably lose a few entrepreneurial individuals who felt constrained by the corporate parent. But overall, you would end up with a workplace where each person, including upper management, felt empowered and where his or her abilities were fully appreciated and used to full advantage.

Personal Branding at the corporate level is a culture change. In a way, I see it as breeding meritocracy: those with talents or expertise become known and their abilities used, while those without anything that brings definable value to the company will be revealed, given help or replaced. You could say that Personal Branding in this milieu is the ultimate truth-telling: who are you, what do you do, and how can you help us?

Seen this way, it's clear that the concept is not something for corporate executives to fear, but to embrace. A Personal Branding culture gives management greater knowledge of people's abilities, and therefore greater control and an ability to plan and implement initiatives. On the employee side, it allows individuals to gain recognition for what they do well and advance based on their performance, rather than on politics. Of course, it's absurd to think that Personal Branding will exterminate the company brown-noser or ambition-driven jerk. It won't. But it can do a lot.

In a time when corporations have made it painfully clear to their people that the halcyon days of lifetime employment and loyalty are but a memory, encouraging a Personal Branding culture is a great way to create that vital esprit d'corps. Instead of giving employees security, companies give them the tools to reinvent themselves and go as far as their talents can take them. That's not a bad alternative.

I strongly believe in Peter Montoya's essential message: Personal Branding is an organic, unavoidable part of today's world. With this book, he gives entrepreneurs, employees and companies the insight and tools to make Personal Branding an ally. That's revolution.

James Speros
Chief Marketing Officer, United States
Ernst & Young

The Personal Branding Phenomenon

In a noisy, information-saturated world, Personal Brands are the new currency of business and culture.

Think about golf, and images spring to mind: emerald fairways, gleaming white balls, quartets of men in ill-considered pants, the hushed tones of a television announcer. Now think of the face of golf. If you're under forty, chances are it's the face of Tiger Woods.

Eldrick "Tiger" Woods was branded long before he became known as a golf prodigy. His father nicknamed him Tiger as a child, in honor of a Vietnamese soldier his father had befriended. When Tiger appeared on the *Mike Douglas Show* at age two, putting with Bob Hope, shot forty-eight for nine holes at age three and appeared in *Golf Digest* at age five, an innocent nickname took on new meaning. By the time he had captured the United States Amateur title in 1994, 1995 and 1996 and won the NCAA title while at Stanford, his name had already become legend on the Professional Golfers Association Tour. Already, he was branded.

The rest is history. The promise of the nickname turned into reality when in 1997, at the age of twenty-one, Woods became the youngest Masters champion ever. But well before that, Tiger Inc., was on its way. Woods's reputation as an amateur, his ethnicity (a blend of African-American, Native-American, Thai and Caucasian backgrounds), personality and youth made him white-hot property to sports, apparel and car companies looking to reach an untapped market: youth golf. They quickly made Woods a multi-millionaire and one of the most famous faces in the world. Before he even won a pro tournament, Tiger Woods *was* the face of golf to a generation raised on computers, hip hop, Nike and Michael Jordan.

No Longer Just a Star, but a Brand

If you doubt that times have changed, contrast the tale of Tiger Woods with that of the man who dominated golf before Woods was even a twinkle in his father's eye: Jack Nicklaus. "The Golden Bear" has long been considered golf's greatest player, with twenty "majors" titles (majors are the United States Open, PGA Championship, British Open and Masters) and seventy PGA Tour wins.

So why didn't Nicklaus become a commercial and media icon like Woods? Because his was a different age, less media-saturated, certainly less marketing-driven. He was a star, no question. But was he someone who represented qualities, values or a culture on a grander scale? Outside the small world of golf, no.

This is a different time. Tiger Woods, and every other major figure in sports, entertainment, the arts, politics, business, religion and human affairs, exist in a world where their brand is as important to their success as who they are as people. And like it or not, so do you.

Welcome to the Age of Personal Branding.

The Branding Craze

Branding has always been around. Companies have always worked to create an aura around their products to make them more desirable. But only in the past twenty years has branding become the dominant concept in marketing, and a science unto itself. In that short time, a powerful, compelling brand has come to be regarded as the key to customer loyalty. A vast advertising and marketing industry has taken root around the challenge of discovering the link between the intangible qualities that make a brand attractive and the revenue produced by that brand.

In the *American Journal of Economics and Sociology*, consumer theorist and university professor Wolfgang Grassl states that consumers perceive brand equity as: "The value added to a product by associating it with a brand name and other distinctive characteristics." Building consumer loyalty, then, becomes a matter of making consumers familiar with products that invoke strong, favorable and unique perceptions for them.

Most buying decisions are based on emotions, not rationality. We find a car, a stereo or a pair of shoes that produces a strong visceral reaction, then we justify our purchasing decision with logic. So, if a brand evokes strong emotions—comfort, familiarity, trust and confidence—in its target consumer, he is more likely to buy. More importantly, the consumer will buy repeatedly—often unprompted by expensive advertising. That's *brand loyalty*. Once a consumer has developed loyalty to a brand, it's all but impossible to erase that brand identity from his mind. For example, consumers still rank General Electric second as a maker of kitchen blenders...twenty years after it stopped making them.

Living in the Over-Information Age

Blame the media—everyone does. But in this case, it's true. The Age of Personal Branding is a creation of the media—spawned by it, nurtured by it, fed by it. In Nicklaus' day, there were three television networks. There was no Internet. Media conglomerates were gleams in the eyes of mergers and acquisitions lawyers.

Today, behemoths like AOL Time Warner and Viacom have demanding shareholders and a bottomless hunger for content—on television, CD, the Internet or the newsstand. There are hundreds of cable channels, scores of independent film companies and an Internet that's becoming a force for cultural change. We have twenty-four-hour cable news, news magazine shows, celebrity news shows and specialty periodicals for everything from "trance" music to trainspotting.

We also have an obsession with people and their "inside" stories. How else could A&E's *Biography*, reality television and exploitative talk shows become cultural engines? We're information junkies shooting up the Information Age.

"Consumers have always been fascinated by people—celebrity kings and queens, presidents and their wives, Hollywood stars—it's a form of voyeurism, an imaginary play with 'possible lives,'" says Dr. Susan Fournier, associate professor of Business Administration at the Harvard Business School and a specialist in relationships between consumers and brands. "Maybe our increasing fascination with the lives of others is a reaction to the loss of close ties in our own social lives. Maybe it's just something that's been supercharged by enabling technologies. Maybe it's an unavoidable consequence of the evolution of a materialist culture and its continuous search for authenticity. Whatever the causes, in today's postmodern culture, we seem to be creating more domains where people can be 'celebritized.' We can't get enough."

With the staggering financial stakes involved, these companies have become as much marketing machines as media distributors. And what sells that content more effectively than anything else? Personalities. People likely to buy from other people with whom they feel some sort of connection. That impulse lies at the heart of the Personal Branding phenomenon.

Familiarity in an Unfamiliar World

Time was, we knew the people who sold us goods, who gave us news. We met them at the corner store, read their columns in the daily paper and then shook their hand in the neighborhood pub. We came to trust their names, faces and reputations.

In today's world, we buy books online, get news from television anchors who have never set foot inside journalism school, and are blitzed with thousands of marketing messages every day. We tune most of them out and regard the rest with indifference or hostility. We're a busy, cynical, frazzled culture with little time to ourselves...and we're sick to *death* of being sold to.

In this environment, the Personal Brand was inevitable. One thing hasn't changed about us: we need to trust that a purchase is right, have a comfort level with the product or identify with the seller before we make that synaptic connection that says, "I'll buy it!" But when a store is owned by a $15 billion holding company, what can we trust?

The Personal Brand. Strong brands instantly communicate simple, clear feelings or ideas to us about a product, company or person. The best corporate brands, like Coca-Cola, evolve over the years to represent the values the seller desires. But most of us distrust the sales pitch of a corporation; we know they're just out for our money. But when the pitch comes from Oprah Winfrey or Bill Cosby? Trust, comfort and identification skyrocket.

Companies have known this for decades, which is why celebrities have been endorsing products since there have been celebrities. But in the twenty-first century, we're not talking about celebrity as spokesperson, but celebrity as product. In fact, we're talking about a human being as product. That's what the Personal Branding phenomenon is really about.

Guarantee-Oriented Society

We live in a guarantee-oriented society. We demand guaranteed jobs, income, sustenance, insurance and relationships (known as marriages). We want guarantees on our cars, our household appliances and just about everything else. A brand taps this need by cloaking a product or person in the illusion of a guarantee. It takes away the perception of risk, implying that when you purchase this product, it will perform. The power of brands to offer certainty in an uncertain world is one of the driving factors behind the phenomenon.

How Personal Branding Affects You

You already have a Personal Brand. Every person does. In your profession, industry or area of expertise, your Personal Brand has grown like a pearl inside an oyster, built from the layers of your behavior, treatment of others, the results of your work and the things you say. Over time, a blend of image, identity and reputation combine to create simple, clear perceptions about you in others. Blend others' hard-to-shake perceptions of you, the instant labels they attach to you and the consistent expectations that follow you, and you have your Personal Brand.

Your Personal Brand affects you in more ways than you realize:

- Whether you are considered for a job opening or other opportunities

- How credible your ideas and statements are

- The amount of effort subordinates will put out for you

- How seriously you're taken by your competition

- The goodwill or ill will of others

- The perceived quality of the service you give or the product you make

- The power (or lack thereof) of your endorsement

- Whether you are seen as different from competitors in your field

- Whether people are willing to pay you what you're worth

Personal Branding Is Strategic

Here's the rub: most people are branded *accidentally*. They have no idea that they've been developing a brand over time, so they fail to capitalize on their brand's strengths and continue to be sabotaged by its weaknesses. This book is all about building a Personal Brand *intentionally*.

Personal Branding is about taking control of the processes that affect how others perceive you, and managing those processes strategically to help you achieve your goals. Our cultural icons leave little to chance—relying on marketing agencies, personal advisors and publicists to groom their brand with precision. Anyone can do the same.

Personal Branding Demands Brutal Honesty

Our greatest challenge is to look in the mirror and objectively evaluate ourselves. It takes courage to render oneself completely vulnerable. However, such brutal self-analysis is the most critical skill in Personal Brand development. As we'll discuss, creating a lasting, great Personal Brand requires absolute authenticity, including the ability to publicly acknowledge weaknesses. Unfortunately, too many individuals try to hide their peccadilloes or worse, go on the attack. Personal Branding demands that every practitioner be prepared for challenging, honest self-evaluation.

WHAT A PERSONAL BRAND IS NOT

A Personal Brand Is Not a Personal Image

Without strategy, all you have is a *personal image*. These days, there are plenty of books and consultants telling you how to build your own brand for career success. But what most of these sources are really telling you to create is a personal image—the exterior packaging for your personal skills and goals. They talk about the car you drive, the clothes you wear, what your business card says and so on. The focus is largely on the tools you should use to get ahead at work.

This approach omits one very important bit of information: *how* and *why* Personal Branding works. Most books in this field drone on about determining the reader's passions, goals and strongest traits. But these are things most people already know and can list in ten minutes. Why spend so much time breaking down the process? The critical step is *understanding* how we perceive others, how those perceptions affect our behavior, and how those same perceptions can be managed in a beneficial way.

When you have that understanding, you can create a Personal Brand and wield it with the dexterity of an orchestra conductor with his baton. Until you do, you're just building a personal image and hoping to get a few notes right.

A Personal Brand Is Not a Person

projection of aspects personality

A Personal Brand is the public *projection* of certain aspects of a person's personality, skills or values; it's not the entire human being. Confusing the two often causes people to fear that they must give up being a real person in exchange for creating a Personal Brand, which isn't the case. A Personal Brand is the enduring perception of the person, not the actual person.

You Are the Source

In the Personal Branding vocabulary, the *source* is the human being behind the Personal Brand—the originator of the carefully packaged and projected public identity. For example, there's Oprah! the Personal Brand, media magnate and idol of millions of women. Then there's Oprah Winfrey the source, brilliant businesswoman. One is public, the other private.

The source must work to fulfill the promises implied by his or her Personal Brand, making the decisions that drive the brand's movement and direction, while keeping his or her own private life separate from the public Personal Brand.

A Personal Brand Is Not Self-Help

This is *not* a self-help book. You will not learn how Personal Branding will help you balance your checkbook, rekindle the passion in your marriage, find your spiritual center, lose thirty-five pounds, rediscover your inner child, adjust your *chakras* or achieve inner peace. This book is about taking control of the branding process and making it work on your behalf.

A More Advanced Approach

The Personal Branding Phenomenon reveals the science and method inside the Personal Brand—the psychological and societal reasons it works, and the eight inviolable laws that underpin every great Personal Brand. It also provides practical information—the benefits of a strong Personal Brand, how to determine the effects of a current, unintentional brand, and a how-to guide to developing and maintaining a Personal Brand.

Most importantly, this advanced look "under the hood" will make you, as a motivated individual or professional marketer, smarter—smarter about how perceptions become reality, smarter about looking past packaging to discover the person behind the brand, and smart enough to realize the need for 100 percent authenticity.

Ready?

Part One:
Personal Branding 101

CHAPTER ONE

Define Your Brand or Your Brand Will Define You

Personal Branding has always existed, but the key to success lies in taking control of this natural, inevitable process.

The workplace has changed radically since the days when one could count on staying with the same company for forty years and retiring with a gold watch and comfy pension. These days, corporations beholden to the bottom line are apt to downsize and restructure any time the mood strikes them—or when Wall Street demands it.

In this world, there's little or no job security, so people have started changing the rules. Rather than be defined by their careers, they've defined themselves by becoming their own one-person enterprise—a Personal Brand. Instead of waiting for opportunities to come to them, they're attracting and creating new ones by taking control of how they're perceived. It is this kind of self-determination that has fueled the growth of the "freelance nation."

We're Already Branded

Each of us already has a Personal Brand—in our family, social circles and profession. We didn't know we were creating it, but it has been building for years. It is the sum total of our achievements, attitudes, actions and treatment of others over time. The more frequent that behavior, the more ingrained it is in the brand.

Want a fairly accurate picture of your Personal Brand? How are you introduced to others? That's a dead giveaway. More revealing is what your friends, family and colleagues say about you when you're not around; if you could poll the people in your domains, you'd get a clear picture of your Personal Brand. Following are the most common characteristics by which people are branded:

- Personality
- Abilities
- Profession
- Interests
- Accomplishments
- Appearance
- Possessions
- Friends
- Lifestyle

There's an advantage to having an existing Personal Brand: you can leverage the strengths of that "accidental" Personal Brand in creating a strategic one. Of course, there's a disadvantage: brand baggage. If a brand has been projecting undesirable ideas into the minds of its audience, it's a long, uphill battle to erase them. Once the mind is made up, it's almost impossible to change it.

WHAT IS A PERSONAL BRAND?

Coke, Volvo and Microsoft each have a "brand essence" that communicates something elemental—not about what they are, but about what they want our perceptions and expectations of them and their products to be.

Any brand is the sum of the expectations and associations it creates in the minds of its audience. It is an implied covenant between product and consumer, a promise that creates a lasting belief in the buyer: "When I buy this, I will be getting this." By communicating with its audience using carefully crafted *response cues* that stimulate strong reactions, a brand creates perceptions that are extremely difficult to alter. With corporate brands, those lasting perceptions are called *brand equity*, and companies spend big bucks building it to ensure that in a crowded marketplace, customers will choose their products.

A Personal Brand works in the same way—communicating values, personality and ideas about ability to its audience to produce a response, then reinforcing that response with more contact. It, too, implies a promise and creates belief in the audience, such as, "When I see Michael Jordan play basketball, he will dominate."

How each person reacts to a Personal Brand is a crapshoot, but the message and intended effect of the brand are always consciously controlled.

Simply put, a great Personal Brand* is:

A personal identity that stimulates precise, meaningful perceptions in its audience about the values and qualities that person stands for.

All the precise definitions in the world can't change one fact: Personal Branding is an inexact science because it involves *subjective* human perceptions. A Personal Brand is like a piece of classical music on the page: it may be finished, but it's not fully realized until it reaches the ears of its audience through performance. And, as even the first violin at the London Symphony Orchestra can play a flat C, sending a Personal Brand into the world can have unexpected effects.

Is Personal Branding the Ultimate in Cynicism?

In a *Fast Company* interview about her book, *No Logo: Taking Aim at the Brand Bullies*, author and activist Naomi Klein worries about

---

*For more essential Personal Branding definitions, see www.petermontoya.com

the prospect of people turning themselves into brands. "Being a brand teaches you to turn every part of yourself into a marketable product," she says. "You're looking for your 'braggables' and for what people can do for you. But ultimately, that's isolating." In an age when corporate brands are often a substitute for culture, and marketing is regarded with increasing suspicion and cynicism, Personal Branding seems to be utterly dehumanizing.

It doesn't have to be. It is what you make of it. Is a Personal Brand manipulative? Not really. It is simply managing a process that's happening anyway and turning it to your advantage. Ironically, Klein has built a powerful Personal Brand for herself by speaking against the evils of brands. Is Klein manipulating us? No. She is building an identity to help her further promote her message.

The Personal Brand you create need not be slick, shallow and deceptive, because the best Personal Brands always reflect the true character of the person behind them. Brands built on lies inevitably crash and burn; just ask Jim Bakker. A Personal Brand built on the person's true character, values, strengths and flaws is a brand that person can live with.

Great Brand vs. Powerful Brand

This book is about building a *great* Personal Brand, not a *powerful* one. What's the difference? A great Personal Brand carries with it a sense of goodwill, virtue or positive value for the audience.

A powerful brand, in contrast, has no such moral compass. It is about power for power's sake. A good example is Oracle chairman Larry Ellison. Clearly, he has a pervasive, powerful brand. But because he is perceived as being power-hungry, egocentric and greedy, he has little goodwill in the minds of the public. Ellison has a powerful Personal Brand, not a *great* one. Great Personal Brands can be powerful, but powerful ones lack that positive edge.

Characteristics, Attributes and the Leading Attribute

Branding, personal or corporate, is a matter of rooting out the aspects of a brand that are most likely to produce powerful responses in the chosen audience. Building a truly great Personal Brand means identifying its key characteristics, refining those into attributes and finally, selecting a leading attribute that anchors the brand.

A characteristic is any basic quality of a Personal Brand: age, height, weight, skill, ethnic background, personality type, education and so on. Characteristics are general qualities that do not imply overt benefits to their domain. Any potential Personal Brand can have hundreds of characteristics. But when beginning the brand building process, it is important to winnow them down to those that are most obvious, distinctive and relevant to the target audience.

For example, the top ten characteristics of Michael Jordan's Personal Brand (in no particular order) would probably be:

1. Charismatic
2. Handsome
3. African-American
4. Jumps high
5. Athletically gifted

6. Skilled basketball player
7. Team leader
8. Ultra-competitive
9. Hard working
10. Commercial spokesman

combine

Take all the general characteristics of a Personal Brand, distill and combine them until you've got a few that create a perception of benefit or value to the target audience, and you have **attributes**. Every great Personal Brand has three to five attributes that are very clear to anyone who becomes familiar with that brand.

distill

Attributes 3-5

Michael Jordan's attributes would most likely be:

1. Great athlete

2. Ultra-competitive champion

3. Prominent African-American

4. Handsome

5. Charismatic spokesman

The **leading attribute** is the most powerful attribute of a Personal Brand. It is usually the perceptual label that enters a person's mind instantly when he encounters a Personal Brand. Michael Jordan's leading attribute is obviously:

The Greatest Basketball Player of All Time

Attributes are the most important building blocks of Personal Brands. In a world of message overload, uncovering and promoting the leading attribute is the best way to give the audience a crystal-clear sense of what makes a Personal Brand unique—it is the difference between greatness and mediocrity. The hard part? Picking just one leading attribute. Too many companies make the error of promoting multiple attributes to win over as many people as possible. The result is confusion.

Audience and Domain

A Personal Brand's **audience** is everyone who is aware of the brand. But it is an imprecise measure, so savvy brand developers must determine the *domain* where their brand will operate.

The **domain** is the sphere of influence—a group of people, companies or organizations with a common association or connection—in which a Personal Brand is established. Selecting the right domain should be a simple matter of asking, "In what arena do I want to achieve my goals?" Choose a domain where you have experience, expertise, knowledge, resources and contacts.

Accomplishments within one domain shape the perception of an entire audience. A Personal Brand should be built for maximum achievement in one domain, because accomplishment will reverberate through a much larger audience. For example, the author of a best-selling business book will not only be recognized by the business community, but by the media, the publishing industry and other authors.

Possible domains:

- Family
- Company
- Industry
- Media
- Nation

- Peers
- Profession
- Community
- Locality
- World

Growing into New Domains

A man sets out to establish his Personal Brand as the most productive salesman anyone has ever seen. Soon, word about his productivity gets out, and he's asked to speak at sales conventions. Suddenly, his Personal Brand has grown from the domain he knows to a new and unknown one: efficiency expert and speaker.

When crafting a brand, ask yourself if it has the potential to grow into other domains. If so, are you willing to let it? If not, be prepared to stop the growth by turning down opportunities. As a brand affects more domains, it becomes harder to maintain its integrity and meet its demands. If you choose the new domain because it's potentially more rewarding, you'll be creating a new Personal Brand very nearly from scratch.

PERSONAL BRANDS ALL AROUND US

Our culture loves Personal Brands. We celebrate and analyze them in the most public ways possible, increasing their influence. We love to rank them, to debate whose influence is greatest and who has fallen from the Olympus of power.

Personal Brands are objects of fascination, which explains the profusion of "most powerful" lists published annually by periodicals from *The Sporting News* to *Premiere*. These lists rank the 100 biggest power brokers in Hollywood, the 100 mightiest names in sports and so on. But what they really rank is the influence of Personal Brands.

Personal Brands are about power and influence, and whether the people named in these lists are branded to the world or just in their field, they've built a Personal Brand that makes them larger than life to the audience they want to influence.

The Sporting News 100 Most Powerful—The Top 20 in 2000

1. Tiger Woods

2. Paul Tagliabue, *NFL Commissioner*

3. Rupert Murdoch, *CEO, News Corp.*

4. David Stern, *NBA Commissioner*

5. Phil Knight, *Nike Chairman and CEO*

6. George Steinbrenner, *principal owner, New York Yankees*

7. Mark McCormack, *founder and CEO, IMG*

8. Bud Selig, *Major League Baseball Commissioner*

9. August Busch IV and Anthony T. Ponturo, *Anheuser-Busch*

10. Dick Ebersol, chairman, *NBC Sports and NBC Olympics*

11. Charles and James Dolan, *Cablevision*

12. George Bodenheimer, *chairman, ESPN*

13. Donald Fehr, *executive director, Major League Baseball Players Association*

14. Sean McManus, *president, CBS Sports*

15. Gary Bettman, *commissioner, NHL*

16. Steve Case, *chairman, AOL Time Warner*

17. Juan Antonio Samaranch, *president, International Olympic Committee*

18. Paul Beeston, *COO, Major League Baseball*

19. Chase Carey, *chairman/CEO, Fox Televsion*

20. Bill France, Jr., *chairman of NASCAR and ISC*

Probably the only familiar names on that list are Tiger Woods and George Steinbrenner. But in their sphere of influence, they are powerful Personal Brands. A Personal Brand is not about being famous. It is about influence.

2001 Forbes Celebrity 100–Top 20

1. Tom Cruise, *actor*

2. Tiger Woods, *golfer*

3. Beatles, *aging musicians*

4. Britney Spears, *pop star*

5. Bruce Willis, *actor*

6. Michael Jordan, *basketball star*

7. Backstreet Boys, *pop group*

8. N'Sync, *pop group*

9. Oprah Winfrey, *multi-media star*

10. Mel Gibson, *actor*

11. Mike Tyson, *boxer*

12. George Lucas, *director*

13. Stephen King, *novelist*

14. Steven Spielberg, *director*

15. Michael Schumacher, *director*

16. Julia Roberts, *actress*

17. Shaquille O'Neal, *basketball player*

18. Metallica, *rock band*

19. Eddie Murphy, *actor*

20. J.K. Rowling, *novelist*

How did *Forbes* capture the essence of celebrity? It ranked these folks according to their income and the media buzz they generate. Many of these names are familiar, but others are hardly in the public eye, or are on the downside of their careers. The Beatles broke up in 1970. Eddie Murphy and Bruce Willis have seen better days. And who is J.K. Rowling? Only the woman who writes the *Harry Potter* books.

Again, having an effective Personal Brand is not about fame, although some of these people certainly have that. It is about what your name, image and influence can make happen in your domain. These people make millions for other people as well as themselves, which is why they are huge.

WHAT A PERSONAL BRAND DOES*

Ultimately, Personal Branding is about influence—the power to influence others' decisions, purchases or attitudes. Some distinct benefits of a great Personal Brand:

- **Confers "top of mind" status:** When someone thinks about a project or opportunity where you are one of numerous candidates, your name is one of the first that comes to mind.

- **Increases the authority and credence of decisions:** A position as an expert within a domain means that statements or decisions are more likely to be believed and carried out.

- **Places you in a leadership role:** A strong Personal Brand encourages people to put you in charge. Federal Reserve Board Chairman Alan Greenspan has a Personal Brand as the wizard of the economy, and the whole country looks to him to keep things booming.

*For a step-by-step guide to putting your professional or entrepreneurial brand into practice, visit www.petermontoya.com and click "Free Information" for a free download, or call (886) 288-9300.

- **Enhances prestige:** Prestige can stem from accomplishments, position, knowledge or even personal style. It gives your actions more weight and increases your visibility.

- **Attracts:** This is one of Personal Branding's strongest powers: the ability to create a personal "aura" that attracts the right people. Look at the Personal Brand of Secretary of State Colin Powell: honest, noble, a leader. In 1996, Powell had no interest in running against Bill Clinton, yet he had to beat the Republican nomination off with a stick. He didn't pursue the opportunity; his Personal Brand *attracted* it.

- **Adds perceived value to what you are selling:** A Personal Brand that conveys honesty, knowledge and intelligence will enhance sales as the customer perceives that the relationship with the person adds value.

- **Earns recognition:** Recognition is not just a matter of ego. It is a matter of credit and opportunities. Great Personal Brands are hard to hide, and if your stamp is on a project or product, people will know it. Anonymity is not the goal.

- **Association with a trend:** A Personal Brand can position you as being part of a hot business methodology or technology. Linus Torvald was a gifted but anonymous programmer in Finland when e-business boomed. Suddenly, the computer operating system he created, Linux, became the cool alternative to Windows. Today he is a guru.

- **Increases earning potential:** By incorporating some or all of these other benefits, a Personal Brand can fuel promotions, boost sales or increase the perception of your expertise so you can demand greater compensation.

WHAT A PERSONAL BRAND WILL NOT DO

- **Cover up incompetence:** One of the core principles of Personal Branding is that you must be highly skilled or knowledgeable in the domain where you are building your brand. If you are a bungler, it will come out. Not only will a Personal Brand not hide incompetence, it will make the consequences worse.

- **Make you famous:** Fame is usually an accident, and it is certainly not a ticket to success. Your Personal Brand is about influencing key people in your domain, not fame for fame's sake. If you become well-known as a side effect, great. But it is not what a Personal Brand is all about.

- **Get you to your goals:** Your Personal Brand on its own will not put your goals on your doorstep. You have also got to set the right goals within your domain, maintain a level of excellence at what you do, actively promote your brand and be consistent over time. A Personal Brand is not a magic bullet.

The Eight Laws

We will be discussing the Eight Unbreakable Laws of Personal Branding throughout this book, starting with the Personal Brand Profile at the end of this chapter. In building a brand, the laws are most useful as continuing reminders of the qualities your brand should develop. Let's define them:

1. **The Law of Specialization.** Focus your brand on one area of achievement.

2. **The Law of Leadership.** You must be acknowledged as one of the most knowledgeable, respected or skilled in your field.

3. **The Law of Personality.** A brand must be built around one's personality in all its aspects, including flaws.

4. **The Law of Distinctiveness.** Once you have created your Personal Brand, you must express it in a unique way.

5. **The Law of Visibility.** To be effective, your Personal Brand must be seen repeatedly.

6. **The Law of Unity.** Your behavior behind closed doors must match your public brand.

7. **The Law of Persistence.** Once you establish your Personal Brand, give it time to grow, stick with it and ignore fads.

8. **The Law of Goodwill.** The more you are perceived as well-intentioned or embodying valued ideals, the more influential your brand.

These Eight Laws are the building blocks of every successful Personal Brand. They are not integral parts of the process of building a Personal Brand or a Personal Brand Statement; rather, they serve as eight yardsticks against which you can measure a Personal Brand as it evolves.

Is your new Personal Brand specialized enough? Has it changed since its launch and lost some of its visibility? Have you violated the Law of Persistence by giving in to temptation and changing your brand? The Laws are the standards, to be considered as you are creating a Personal Brand and used to check its development over time.

Personal Brand Profile

Martha Stewart
The World's Homemaker

Martha Stewart is the symbol of all things gracious and beautiful in the home. Through her growing empire of television, magazines, books and retail presence, Stewart has built a Personal Brand identity that is simple and extraordinarily powerful: the fount of all knowledge about how to make the perfect home.

Martha Stewart [1941 –   ]

Born Martha Kostyra, on August 3, 1941, in New Jersey, Stewart grew up in Nutley, New Jersey, and worked as a model from the age of thirteen. After attending Barnard College and earning a degree in European and architectural history, she married Andy Stewart, a Yale law student, in 1961. Six years later, she began working as a stockbroker for Monness, Williams, and Sidel and stayed until 1972, when the family moved to Westport, Connecticut.

After restoring their nineteenth-century farmhouse, Stewart decided to focus her energy on gourmet cooking. She started a catering business in the late 1970s, and within a decade, Martha Stewart, Inc., had grown into a $1 million business serving corporate and celebrity clients. Stewart followed this with her first book, *Entertaining*, which became a bestseller and was followed by Martha *Stewart's Quick Cook Menus*, *Martha Stewart's Hors d'Oeuvres*, *Martha Stewart's Christmas* and *Martha Stewart's Wedding Planner*. An empire built on fine food and fine living had begun.

How This Brand Was Built

Harvard University's, Dr. Susan Fournier, who has produced many detailed case studies on powerful Personal Brands including Stewart's, points out that Stewart's prodigious brand is an example of perfect timing. Fournier says that in the feminist 1970s, when home and hearth were rejected by women in favor of career, Stewart's ideas would have been utterly rejected.

"She waited for the time to come, for the Super Mom myth to explode," says Fournier. "The culture was ready for her whole brand meaning. It's more savvy than luck, but there is some luck involved."

As cultural tides turned back toward family and home, Stewart was turning her culinary knowledge and home restoration experience into a vision: selling the beautification and refinement of the home and garden. When she realized that her vision could only become widespread with the synergy of a periodical and a television show, she found a partner in Time Warner and began publishing a magazine, *Martha Stewart Living*, in 1991. Her syndicated television show of the same name launched in 1993, and Martha Stewart Omnimedia came to be in 1996. Today, with a presence in K-Mart and other stores, more than twenty books, and a public company, the savvy, opportunistic caterer has built an industry.

Why This Brand Works

- **Extension:** Stewart has a presence in nearly every medium: television, magazines, books, radio, retail. Her high level of visibility increases the perception of her expertise even as it makes more and more people aware of what she offers.

- **Authority:** Stewart states of her enterprise, "We are the leading authority for the home." And she is perceived as exactly that. Being the first major player in the home beautification business has made her the definitive source for tips on cooking, decorating, gardening, you name it.

- **Control:** Stewart is known as a take-no-prisoners leader, one who exercises total control over her empire. She guards her image ferociously and has the final say over most of what happens under her name—critical for maintaining brand consistency.

- **Appeal:** She is selling the home: making it more beautiful, cooking better food, creating a more beautiful garden, making the holidays more special. There is no negative to what Stewart is selling, even though her critics deride her for promoting impossible standards. Home, hearth and warmth have near-universal appeal.

Adherence to the Eight Laws

1. **The Law of Specialization.** Her first-mover advantage has established her as the first person to think of what she is selling, even if she's not.

2. **The Law of Leadership.** Her name has become synonymous with gracious, elegant, upscale homemaking and decorating.

3. **The Law of Personality.** She has built her brand and her empire on a genuine early interest in the culinary arts and in home restoration, having restored her now-famous Turkey Hill farmhouse.

4. **The Law of Distinctiveness.** She has not done everything she can to distinguish herself from others in the same field, but she doesn't need to. Her reach is so much wider and her presence so much larger, she eclipses any copycats.

5. **The Law of Visibility.** Her cross-media presence is astonishing. Along with Oprah, she is the most visible businesswoman in the United States.

6. **The Law of Unity.** She guards her privacy religiously, and there is some sense that her smiling visage and homey manner are less than genuine. So far, it hardly matters.

7. **The Law of Persistence.** Stewart is driven, ambitious and smart, and worked for years to turn her early book publishing success into her multi-media colossus. She has maintained and built on the same brand identity year after year.

8. **The Law of Goodwill.** To some, she is a pernicious cultural force promoting a domestic image as unhealthy and unrealistic as the body images promoted by anorexic models. But to most women, she is symbolic of grace, comfortable living and beautiful surroundings. She inspires tremendous devotion.

Influence in Its Domain

Martha Stewart's ideas have changed how many people look at the home environment. Her ideas and identity have entered the mainstream, and her business success has, along with that of Oprah Winfrey, changed how we look at the potential for the individual as icon. Thanks to her, the individual can be a business, even an industry.

CHAPTER TWO

Selling, Marketing and Branding

In a world sick of being sold to, and tired of being reduced to marketers' data, a Personal Brand is the key to capturing hearts and minds.

Thanks to the ham-handed efforts of a bunch of college boys playing CEO for companies that should have never existed, branding has suffered a black eye. Tell a Wall Street analyst you're trying to build your company's brand and it's about fifty to fifty your share price will crater. Branding's brand has taken a few hits to the chin.

But to the experts, the marketing people at corporations like Procter & Gamble, Coca-Cola and Toyota, brand development isn't a cash-burning free-for-all. It's essential to grabbing and retaining market share—and it takes time, finesse and skill. But it's very real, very powerful and very much sought after.

About 90 percent of corporate marketing professionals can't explain the difference between sales, marketing and branding*. To justify their own existences, or for ad agencies to justify their stratospheric fees, marketing types have concocted complex, arcane definitions for each idea. But when you boil each concept down to its essence, it's quite simple.

---

*To fight sales, marketing and branding ignorance, send the unenlightened to www.petermontoya.com to download this chapter free. Or call (866) 288-9300 and we'll fax it to you.

Sales Is Convincing

Selling is the world's third oldest profession, and the road-weary door-to-door salesman is an American archetype. Sales is the art of persuasion. The salesperson uses questioning tactics, listening skills and mental judo to convince his audience that they simply can't do without his product

If you've ever encountered a really good salesperson, you know from experience that some people just have the gift of persuasion; they can talk you into anything. The truly gifted can respond to your natural sales resistance and get you to talk *yourself* into anything.

That is the key. Selling is *creating a need* where one does not exist, or where the need is too small to stimulate action on its own. In sales, you chase a customer who may not want to listen, and you make him listen. It is the business equivalent of capturing and tagging a wild animal. Sales is not about image or finesse. It is arm-wrestling for dollars, selling pure benefits and price without a thought for the emotional needs of the customer.

"We'll Stand on Our Heads to Sell You This Car."

If you want examples, look at local car dealerships. It's all about price, best terms, "come on down!" There's no subtlety or creative concept behind these commercials; the wackier and wilder the better—so long as you remember them. Their sole purpose is enticing you to come down to the dealership, where the sales staff can work on you in person.

A great example from my native Southern California is Cal Worthington, who has reigned for over three decades as the unabashed king of used-car salesmanship. His antics include "standing on his head until his face turns red" and walking the lanes of his car lot with his "dog" Spot—usually an elephant, bear or tiger. His over-the-top, unapologetic hucksterism draws customers like flies.

And once the sales pitch gets you in the door, you've got a team of sales pros ready to take advantage of your emotional attachment to a certain vehicle. They use old-fashioned "take-give" sales tactics, playing on one universal fact: you didn't come to haggle, you came to buy a car. They can wait you out. Brand advertising may have made the car appealing, but in the dealership it's about pure sales: price, pressure, get the signature.

Marketing Is Generating

Marketing is sales' more glamorous cousin. It is a single term for the collective activities companies use to *generate* business: running ad campaigns, conducting demographic research, buying television commercial time and so on. It is also a dirty word these days for consumers tired of mailboxes filled with credit card offers and their private information sold over the Internet. For plenty of consumers, the idea of marketing is joined at the hip with the specter of corporate greed, and it is an image that has led marketers to be distrusted almost as much as attorneys.

But strip away the baggage and marketing is as simple as its name: the science of creating a market by sending carefully crafted messages to the proper target audience, through multiple channels, over time. Marketing puts a sales message in front of the potential customer using different means, such as radio ads, direct mail and the media. It is planting the seeds of commerce for later cultivation by salespeople and setting the stage for sales by letting the customer know the product exists, including how they should feel about it. Over time, well-executed marketing builds awareness, wears down sales resistance and creates interest.

Marketing produces three levels of response in its audience:

1. **Awareness:** When an audience first comes into contact with a marketing message, awareness is created. People go from being igno-

rant that a product even existed to the knowledge that it does. That is always the first step.

2. **Affinity:** Upon multiple exposures to marketing messages, some people will begin to develop positive feelings toward the brand, even without knowing much about the product. That is why soft drink commercials are so relentlessly upbeat; the marketers want you to feel good about drinking their soda even when you are not drinking it.

3. **Understanding:** Eventually, affinity for a product leads to greater investigation. At this point, good marketing helps a consumer understand how and why the product benefits them or is right for them. The appeal is to the intellect as well as the gut.

Tony Robbins and Personal Power

Self-help guru Anthony Robbins is a great example of using a Personal Brand for a marketing goal. He has turned his overpowering personality, mega-watt smile and positive philosophy into the driving force behind his best-selling books and sold-out seminars. The objective of his books, seminars and infomercials is to sell—and he does so, which is why Robbins is a Personal Marketing* master.

Robbins' tireless *Personal Power* "you can change your life" message has created a billion-dollar Personal Brand with unlimited influence that spans the globe. It's no accident that when professional sports teams like the L.A. Kings and San Antonio Spurs want to motivate their players with a locker room speech, they call on Robbins.

Branding Is Influencing

Whereas marketing is actively presenting an offer to buy, branding is creating an identity that causes others to associate certain qualities, values or feelings with that identity—eventually creating an affinity that leads them to buy. A strong brand is the rock-solid

---

*For more information on Personal Branding's little brother, Personal Marketing, visit www.petermontoya.com and download the Special Report "Personal Marketing v. Personal Branding" or call (866) 288-9300.

foundation for all marketing, because every other aspect of a product's identity—its logo, how its ads are written, who its spokesperson is—is based on that brand. Branding is the reason customers consider a product in the first place.

Personal Branding is about creating a unique personal identity around a leading attribute, managing the perceptions of your audience to make them feel a certain way about you and what you can offer. Like a product brand, a great Personal Brand "pre-sells" people on you, making them aware of your character, strengths and personality before they ever meet you. Great Personal Brands do not necessarily attract sales, but rather, attract power. A Personal Brand gives the power to influence the decisions, attitudes and actions of an audience.

The Dealmaker

The average guy has never heard of Mark McCormack, but in the sports world, his Personal Brand is without peer. A Yale-educated sports agent, promoter and lawyer, McCormack began his career by offering to arrange exhibitions for Arnold Palmer and founded the International Management Group (IMG) in 1962. The agency quickly grew into the largest personal management agency in the world, handling the sponsorship deals and promotion for numerous sports stars and other personalities.

McCormack's and IMG's client lists are a "who's who" of the sports and entertainment world. From Tiger Woods to the Pope, if you want recognition or a great deal on your next contract, Mark McCormack has the influence to make it happen. His Personal Brand attracts huge clients who know his reputation for getting things done on a global scale.

Branding Is Everything

Branding has been mislabeled as advertising. The truth is, branding is *everything*. Everything you do affects your Personal Brand. That includes:

- The way you walk, talk and dress
- Your education, neighborhood and profession
- Your choice of spouse, car and friends
- The way you sell, negotiate and meet your obligations
- Your customer service and presentation skills
- How well you follow through on your promises

Branding is not marketing, advertising or promotion. It's everything.

The Brand Continuum

Brand Widget

Imagine a continuum that goes on infinitely in both directions, using Salesman A from Company A, selling Brand Widget as an example.

Brand Widget

The category of "sales assets" can include sales pitch, personality, physical presentation, personal appearance and negotiating skills.

Brand Widget

Notice that selling is contained as part of marketing. Marketing includes many factors outside the control of Salesman A: product, price, performance, lead generation, advertising, market research, product development and customer service.

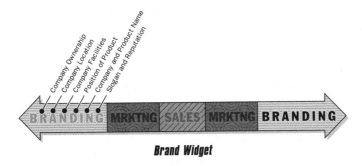

Brand Widget

Notice that both sales and marketing are parts of branding. Branding is everything contained in sales and marketing plus any or all of the following: company ownership, company location, company facilities, position of product, company and product name, slogan and reputation.

Because Branding is everything, sales and marketing help build brands, and vice-versa. In short, everything you do affects your Personal Brand, either by supporting it or contradicting it.

What does that mean? In the Short Attention Span Theater that is our modern world, branding allows us to form impressions instantly as information blurs past us. So, before any new product or service can be sold or marketed, it should be branded. With individuals, developing a compelling Personal Brand is like tilling the soil before planting seeds.

It is possible to sell a product or a person without branding it, but in this message-saturated culture, building a strong, memorable brand makes the process easier, far less costly and more effective in the long term. Our society speaks brand language fluently and embraces a well-constructed Personal Brand more readily than the best resume.

Branding Ain't Easy

Why do so many companies spend so much money to create compelling brands and develop brand equity, and botch it so badly? The key reasons:

1. **Brands take time:** A smart company can put the messages and image in place to create a great brand, but the brand identity always grows over time. Nike is a perfect example of a company building a splendid brand over time, letting the brand identity grow organically within the culture the company was trying to reach.

2. **Branding isn't always rational:** Imagine the first meeting with Nike when ad agency Wieden and Kennedy proposed "Just do it" to a bunch of guys trying to sell shoes. The tagline has nothing to do with shoes, which is why it has become a classic. Instead of trying to build a brand based on the tactile qualities of their shoes— a commodity—Nike built it on striving, sweating and sacrificing to be the best. They ignored the empty claims of sales and focused on hitting customers in the gut.

3. **Brands aren't about ads:** Ever hear the oxymoron "instant classic?" That's when companies try to short-circuit the brand development

process. It is endemic in the youth market: design a product, spend millions on a hip, edgy ad campaign, attach a cool Web site to it, and instant brand equity, right? Wrong. Brands develop based on the product and how it makes people feel, not on the ad campaign.

4. **Brands demand consistency and clarity:** In 2000, Oldsmobile decided to kill its venerable family of autos. Why? Sales were plummeting, partially because of inconsistent brand messaging. No one really knew who the cars were for—young adventurers or retirees? Crown Books filed for bankruptcy in 2001 after two decades as the nation's discount bookstore. Their error: trying to compete with superstores like Barnes & Noble by opening Super Crown. The strategy took them away from their brand strength—low prices. And Royal Crown Cola, which many agree tastes better than Coke or Pepsi, is barely on the soft drink map because it lacks any consistent visibility. Three disastrous examples of inconsistent, unclear branding.

Personal Brand Profile

Jack Welch
The Greatest CEO Ever

Former General Electric CEO Jack Welch is the Obi-Wan Kenobi of CEOs, the man who, during his twenty-year reign, turned a company best known for light bulbs into the dominant force in more than twenty industries, with over $130 billion in revenue in 2000. But what made "Neutron Jack" into an overwhelming Personal Brand was his vision. He steered GE away from manufacturing into the insanely profitable service business, and embraced the Internet before almost anyone else. He is an icon, regarded not just as one of the best CEOs of his generation, but in history.

Jack Welch (1935 –   )

John Francis Welch Jr. was born in Salem, Massachusetts in 1935. A 1957 graduate of the University of Massachusetts with a B.S. in chemical engineering, Welch continued to pursue his education at the University of Illinois, earning his master's and doctorate in the science.

Welch joined General Electric in 1960, but initially the marriage was not made in heaven. After one year, Welch contemplated leaving GE to take a job at International Minerals & Chemicals. Working as a junior engineer in Pittsfield, Massachusetts, for a salary of $10,500, Welch felt underpaid and stifled by GE's strict bureaucracy. An executive, who saw hints of Welch's future greatness, spent four hours convincing him to stay…and a legendary CEO was on his way.

How This Brand Was Built

Critical to the greatness of Welch's brand has been his ability to render himself and GE synonymous. There was never a doubt about who was at the helm and responsible for the massive changes in the company. This high profile also earned him respect for being willing to put his own neck on the line.

Just as critical was Welch's vision. Ruthless and audacious, he insisted that in each of its businesses, GE be either number one or number two. If a business fell short, it was sold or shut down. The result: over 130,000 layoffs, over seventy plant closings, and a $500 billion increase in shareholder value.

A third key to Welch's brand is his passion, both for excellence in corporate operations, and for teaching young GE managers. Accessibility, charisma and a willingness to pass on his wisdom have branded him as more than a ruthless CEO.

Finally, Welch continued to build his Personal Brand by going out on top, retiring at age sixty-five when he could have stayed on until he dropped. His reward: a $7.1 million advance for his biography.

Why This Brand Works

- **Excellence:** Welch turned GE into the world's most valuable company—more profitable, agile, and ready to dominate in the Information Age. He did everything he promised and more.

- **Authority:** Welch's success has elevated him to the position of Über-CEO, the man other CEOs go to when they need answers. No one else is even close.

- **Flaws:** Welch never tried to conceal his flaws: his temper, his intolerance for failure, and his slight stutter. Instead of being a corporate emperor, he became more human.

- **Confidence:** Even when colleagues, the media and ex-employees were telling him he was going too far, Welch pressed on, ultimately certain that his way was the right way. Ultimately, he was proved correct.

Adherence to the Eight Laws

1. **The Law of Specialization.** There are plenty of CEOs out there, so it is hard to specialize. But this did not affect his brand; he just became the best in the world.

2. **The Law of Leadership.** No one was seen as more creative, aggressive, forward-thinking or relentless than Welch—and his results speak for themselves.

3. **The Law of Personality.** Welch did not hide his flaws. He had a temper and could not tolerate mediocrity. He balanced these attributes

with charisma and the willingness to be solely responsible for the results of his directives.

4. **The Law of Distinctiveness.** When people refer to a CEO as "another Jack Welch," you know the man stood out. He made everyone else a follower.

5. **The Law of Visibility.** Every business reporter, MBA professor and corporate executive in the western world knows Welch, and since the publication of his autobiography, he is getting even more airtime.

6. **The Law of Unity.** Welch the CEO was Welch the man, for the most part. His ferocious passion for excellence manifested in his obsession with golf, his teaching and his entire life.

7. **The Law of Persistence.** Welch never wavered in his management style, so his Personal Brand maintained its momentum.

8. **The Law of Goodwill.** Shareholders loved him. Labor and laid-off workers loathed him. But Welch followed this law fairly well, because it was known that his intent was to make GE more profitable and competitive.

Influence in Its Domain

Jack Welch was the first modern celebrity CEO, paving the way for Bill Gates, Jeff Bezos, Ted Turner and Nike's Phil Knight. His influence glamorized business leadership, set the stage for the e-business bubble and changed how corporate leadership is viewed.

CHAPTER THREE

How Personal Branding Works

Part psychology, part science and part art– Personal Branding is the alchemy of establishing powerful, lasting perceptions in the human psyche.

In his book *Faster: The Acceleration of Just About Everything*, James Gleick points out that in modern culture, our short attention spans demand such intense and rapid stimulation that anything moderately paced feels unbearably slow. He asks if, as a result of this demand for cognitive hyperactivity, we have, "by way of compensation, traded away our capacity for deep concentration?"

Add to that accelerated pace the constant bombardment of television, radio, film, music, radio, cell phones, e-mail, Internet, work, family, hobbies, church and so on. With brains that are capable of coherently processing only a few thoughts at a time, it is easy to see why we sometimes shut down to avoid the endless bombardment of data.

Judging on Instinct

In such a society, judging others based on immediate visual and behavioral cues becomes habit, then instinct. It is evolutionary baggage from a couple hundred thousand years ago, when humans lived in nomadic, pre-agrarian societies. One of our critical survival skills was the ability to form instantaneous, compelling perceptions about our environment. These perceptions are our cognitive processes and allow us to react to a situation when taking the time to think about it could be deadly.

Today we do the same in the more modern context of a cocktail party. A woman is introduced to a man, and before she shakes his hand, she's forming instant perceptions about him based on his clothing, hair or posture. After she's introduced, she'll make more judgments about him based on his speech and basic personal information. For her, his Personal Brand has begun to coalesce. The way our perceptual abilities have evolved, it's in our nature to quickly label people, objects and situations based on immediate visual and sensory cues.

"I'm not so shallow," you protest. Sure you are. Labeling others based on instant perceptions is automatic in humans. Upon meeting someone, you label them based on some of these questions:

• What do you do?

• Where do you live?

• Are you married?

• Where did you go to school?

• Where are you from?

• What do you drive?

Brand-Building Forces

Just as three elementary particles—electrons, protons and neutrons—are at the heart of every atom, three essential elements make up the heart of every Personal Brand:

1. **Emotional Impact:** In the end, the decision to hire someone, buy a product or award a project is based on a blend of emotional reaction and rational thinking. However, getting a person considered—known as getting them into the *decision set*—is often a matter of how the decision-maker *feels* about the person. A great Personal Brand triggers strong, positive responses in the people in its domain: confidence, admiration, fondness, trust, fascination.

2. **Repetition:** An effective Personal Brand must remain consistent. The goal is to root the brand attributes in the minds of the audience; the only way to do that is with repeated exposure to the same brand message. Change the brand and confusion results, as people are not sure how to feel.

3. **Time:** As we repeatedly encounter and respond to a Personal Brand, instinctive perceptions—associated with the personality traits, values or abilities the person represents—become automatic, and strong enough to drive our actions. But there are no shortcuts. Long-term exposure to the Personal Brand is the only way to form such strong perceptions.

Three Levels of Brand Status

One of the primary reasons people are reluctant to create a Personal Brand is the misguided belief that it is a tool only for the world stage—you have got to be global to be branded. Wrong. A Personal Brand is effective on any scale, from an executive trying to move up the corporate ladder to an advertising agency grooming the perfect spokesperson for a product. The principle of influencing the perceptions of others through branding is valid at any level.

Every Personal Brand exists at one of three levels:

1. **Advocate: the Personal Brand is associated with a trend:** Trends are short-lived changes in the larger culture, and endure for as lit-

tle as one year or as long as seven years. At this level, the Personal Brand does not shape a trend, but taps into it and uses the trend's popularity to increase people's awareness and acceptance of the brand. Example: an architect sees a resurgence of Spanish Revival design in L.A. and re-positions his business to be the "Spanish Revival architect."

The downside to settling for advocate status is this: once the trend plays out, your notoriety goes with it. Tying a Personal Brand to a trend is a good way to build fast awareness and popularity, but it is short-lived.

2. **Trendsetter: the Personal Brand influences trends and is a presence in the larger culture:** This is the ideal state for strong Personal Brands. Trendsetters straddle the line between short-term trends and the culture they occupy (such as the fashion world, software development or law). Trendsetting Personal Brands ride new trends as they come along, but their sources are also deeply engaged in the culture of their domain. When the trend fades, the connection with the culture keeps the Personal Brand relevant. Also, being connected to the larger culture allows the source to see new trends coming and tap their momentum.

Example: Clothing designer Tommy Hilfiger can follow the trend of the moment in creating his fashions. However, because his Personal Brand in the fashion industry is strong, he remains relevant even when he is not in tune with a fast-changing trend, and he can affect and change his culture.

3. **Icon: the Personal Brand is etched into the culture:** This is the rarified air in which world-famous figures reside—people who, through design or achievement, have risen to symbolize an attribute, value or concept in the minds of a vast range of people. Example: Bob

Dylan was the leading figure in socially-aware "protest" music and is still considered the symbol of the movement.

Icon status is beyond most of us, largely because it is out of our hands. Few people set out to become icons; it happens organically, over time. The decision is in the hands of the audience.

Brands Exist in the Mind

The struggle to craft, maintain and promote a great Personal Brand takes place between the ears, in the battle to control perceptions and hold attention. The mind is the battleground competing brands fight over, and the Personal Brand that can evoke the strongest, most lasting perceptions in the mind wins. Different from *brain*, the **mind** is the three-part cognitive state of each human being in a brand's domain: the ability to form perceptions based on stimuli, the status and strength of those perceptions, and the reactions and behaviors they stimulate.

A Personal Brand's effect on the mind is the final step in what consumer psychologists call the *perceptual process*:

1. Perceptions: These are our learned interpretations of basic sensory information, such as the sound waves from an audio source striking the organs in our inner ear to produce sound. We interpret these perceptions without conscious thought, as when we recognize our mother's voice.

2. Attributes: These are more complex interpretations of stimuli that we have learned to associate with a perception. Attributes are a more sophisticated form of understanding in which we use our intellect to interpret and judge incoming information. Example: smelling a perfume and deciding it is too sweet.

3. Gestalts: These are extremely powerful learned perceptions that, over time, have become compelling and automatic. We cannot prevent

the perceptions from occurring, and we need take no conscious action to make them occur. Consequently, Gestalts are crucial in brand development. All perceptions have the potential to become Gestalts as we respond to them repeatedly:

• The Japanese make quality cars.

• Teenagers are difficult.

• Salespeople lie.

Personal Brands Produce Attitudes

A great Personal Brand evokes an emotional response in its audience. But in the end, the deciding factor in the Personal Brand's effectiveness comes down to which of two simple responses it generates: "good" or "bad." A Personal Brand will make each person exposed to it feel a different way—amused, stimulated, challenged, stressed and so on. If that person interprets the feeling as "good," the brand and its source will be regarded positively. If the interpretation is negative, good luck trying to win this person over.

Such personal good/bad interpretations are **attitudes**, and they will have a great deal to do with the success of the Personal Brand you create. Attitudes are largely the result of a simple behavioral equation: BELIEF + VALUE = ATTITUDE. Here is an example:

A segment of the population holds the belief that Jerry Springer hosts the most infamous of the daytime talk shows. This group also holds the value that such talk shows are unmitigated sleaze. Their resulting attitude is that Jerry Springer is the world's leading sleaze-monger.

Individuals often base attitudes on other components, like the perceptions produced by on-the-job performance, or by a recommendation from a trusted source. However, many exposures to a Personal

Brand involve only the basic B + V = A equation, because there is little additional evidence to go on.

The Mind Is Never Wrong

It is an axiom of marketing: the mind is never wrong (the customer is always right). The only solution is to re-launch the brand in a new domain with few perceptions attached with it. It's tough, but it can be done: Ron Howard, wanting to get away from the all-American image he built in such work as *American Graffiti* and *Happy Days*, left acting altogether to become a successful director. An entire generation has now come to maturity never knowing that the director of *Apollo 13* was once known as Opie.

What does this mean to the development of a great Personal Brand? That the Personal Brand you develop should be designed to influence the attitudes your audience develops toward the attributes of the brand—creativity, charm, decisiveness, coolness, funky clothes and so on.

You cannot begin with Gestalts; they take time. But by influencing basic perceptions in the right way, you can help the right Gestalts form. With repeated contact and consistency, perceptions become automatic, powerful and associated with positive feelings. And once those perceptions are set, they will last.

Reading the Culture

One of the most challenging aspects to building a Personal Brand is that its acceptance is out of your control. As Harvard University's Dr. Fournier states, "Branding isn't an imperative, it's a privilege granted by someone else. We think we have this right to brand, and we don't."

Fournier points out that the most successful Personal Brands are created by people attuned to the cultural tides of their domain—people who offer the right brand at the right time. "The best Personal Brands have the ability to read the cultural barometer, what Faith Popcorn calls 'Brailling the culture'," she says. "If you're a sensitive cultural critic, you can identify those times when the culture is hungry for meaning."

You Can't Brand a Lie

Personal Brands are as fragile as bone china. They can be tainted or broken with a single ill-advised sentence. A perfect example is Jimmy Swaggart, the television minister who waged war on sin until he publicly admitted to an unspecified "sin," later alleged to involve a prostitute. Despite his tearful "I have sinned against you" speech and his penitence, he has never rehabilitated his image, so betrayed did many of his followers feel.

And these principles become null and void if a Personal Brand is built on falsehood. It is possible to create Gestalts based on deceptive brand attributes, because if the mind believes it, it's true. But it's dangerous. Give people the slightest hint that they've been misled about a brand and their Gestalts can swing to the other extreme. In other words, if you're caught in a lie, intense positive perceptions can turn intensely negative in seconds. People hate a hypocrite.

Personal Brand Profile

Walt Disney
The Family Entertainment Man

No one did more to change the nature of family entertainment than Walter Elias Disney. He was a visionary who saw virtue in creating an alternate world that embodied all-American values: community, family, tradition and simple pleasures. His passion created an empire, and his name is synonymous with family, animated films and child-like wonder.

Walt Disney (1901-1966)

Disney was born on December 5, 1901 in Chicago, and raised on a farm in Marceline, Missouri, and in Kansas City. Basic art instruction from correspondence courses and Saturday museum classes would later help him turn the animals and people from that Missouri farm into his first animated characters.

At seventeen, Disney dropped out of high school to serve in World War I. Disney returned to Kansas City in 1919 for an apprenticeship as a commercial illustrator. By 1922, he had set up his own cartoon production shop with Ub Iwerks, whose drawing ability and technical inventiveness were prime factors in Disney's eventual success.

Moving to Hollywood in 1923, Disney entered into partnership with his elder brother Roy. His first success was the creation of Mickey Mouse in *Steamboat Willie,* the first fully synchronized sound cartoon. With the invention of new characters and an obsession with technical improvements, Disney was on the road to becoming a household name.

How This Brand Was Built

Disney built his brand largely by doggedly pursuing his clear vision. He defied conventional wisdom in creating *Snow White* as a feature-length animated film, and in opening Disneyland at a time when amusement parks had a tawdry, dangerous image. He also revolutionized the idea of customer service, calling customers "guests," employees "cast members," and insisting that each moment of a guest's experience must be crafted into magic.

Disney also built his brand by being a pioneer. While his brothers ran their animation studio, Walt fostered the development of new technologies such as synchronized sound and Technicolor. Taking risks was part of his philosophy.

Perhaps the final piece in Disney's Personal Brand was his treatment of the people who worked for his organization. Though he could be a demanding employer, he worked hard to avoid layoffs, encouraged employees to pitch their ideas to him and showed a loyalty to them that is unheard of from a chief executive today.

Why This Brand Works

- **Audacity:** Disney did everything big, risky and made it all work. One of his last major projects was the initial plan for Disney World and EPCOT Center, which he did not live to see finished.

- **Confidence:** Disney believed in his vision and never wavered. Of his success he said, "I dream, I test my dreams against my beliefs, I dare to take risks, and I execute my vision to make those dreams come true."

- **Visible name:** Disney battled with animators over personal credit, wanting to release films with only the Disney name. He knew the public's recognition and identification would be greater with a single person who stood for the company. Long before his death, his name came to stand for a set of values.

- **Audience knowledge:** Disney knew his target audience was experiencing a loss of innocence due to the Depression, World War II and the Cold War. He knew what those people needed: magical moments that transported them to another place. And he gave it to them.

Adherence to the Eight Laws

1. **The Law of Specialization.** Disney did it all first, changing the face of animation and amusement parks. Everyone else was a copy.

2. **The Law of Leadership.** It is hard to argue with the statement that Walt knew more about family entertainment than anyone alive. Many say that he was the greatest storyteller in the history of Hollywood.

3. **The Law of Personality.** Disney's warm treatment of his people engendered great loyalty, though his naivete in employment matters did make him some enemies.

4. **The Law of Distinctiveness.** Disney was renowned as a risk-taking visionary who could turn his beliefs into reality. Truly a unique identity.

5. **The Law of Visibility.** The man was the company, and with the company constantly on the world stage thanks to new films or Disneyland, Walt's visibility was sky-high.

6. **The Law of Unity.** Disney in public was Disney in private. He was a fairly guileless man with a true love of small-town America; the loyalty of the people who worked for him is proof of the validity of his image.

7. **The Law of Persistence.** He continued to push the envelope of entertainment right up to the time of his death in 1966.

8. **The Law of Goodwill.** Walt Disney today is still viewed as a kindly father figure thanks to his high visibility on the Disney Channel and the Wonderful World of Disney.

Influence in its Domain

Disney challenged everyone in entertainment to be as innovative as he had. His linking of multiple properties (turning movie characters into Disneyland rides, for example), set the stage for the million-dollar product tie-ins of today. For better or worse, he defined family entertainment in the twentieth century.

Part Two:

The Eight Unbreakable Laws of Personal Branding

CHAPTER FOUR

Law One: The Law of Specialization

Great Personal Brands focus on one area of achievement. Try to be all things to all people and you are nothing to anyone.

Think of Giorgio Armani. Instantly, a mental image of immaculately tailored men's attire comes to mind. Instant identification is one of the most basic aspects of a great Personal Brand: the power to provoke an immediate, reflexive response in the audience, whether it is an emotion, a mental picture or a compulsion to take action.

The Law of Specialization says that a great Personal Brand must be precise, concentrated on a single core strength, talent or achievement. The result of this concentration is the compelling, instantaneous *frisson* of certainty that occurs when people come into contact with a great Personal Brand. For example, Michael Jordan has been a baseball player, a golfer and a spokesman, but he has never "pulled focus" from his Personal Brand as the greatest basketball player ever.

One of the critical tests of a Personal Brand: does it influence others to form a single, quick, desirable perception about you? If not, you may be trying to do too much and risking confusion. People like to feel perceptive. Let them.

Do Less, Be More

The easiest way to avoid confusion about a Personal Brand is to keep surface perceptions simple. The public side of any Personal Brand consists of two levels: the easily identifiable surface and the complexities about ability, performance and character that demand greater time and analysis from an audience. To lead people to examine the deeper levels, a Personal Brand must engage an audience with its clarity and simplicity.

Bob Vila can be summed up in one, clean phrase, "home restoration." The home restoration sensation that made Vila a symbol began with *This Old House*, the PBS program he hosted beginning in 1979. During the restoration of homes throughout New England, Vila's bearded, genial face became associated with a "you can do it" philosophy that infected much of the United States with a do-it-yourself disease. As identified with home renovation as Martha Stewart is with home decorating, Vila polishes his Personal Brand on his show *Bob Vila's Home Again*.

Keep the Personal Brand "Bit Size"

The *bit* is the most basic unit of information: a yes or no answer to one unambiguously phrased question. If the Personal Brand you build is well crafted, people in its domain will be able to respond to questions about its basic nature in a single bit, that is, with a simple yes or no.

Is Steve Jobs, Apple Computer's CEO, the maniacal, innovative leader of the personal computing revolution? Yes. Jobs is celebrated less for his management skill than for bringing back passion and creativity to the company he co-founded in 1976. Alternately described as a pioneer, a visionary and an egotistical jerk, Jobs made his Personal Brand by riding to the rescue in 1996 when he returned to Apple as interim CEO, after a series of dismal quarters and product bombs. Almost immediately, he led the company's resurgence with the release of the iMac, taking on the aura of an evangelical minister. Glib, bold and highly visible, Jobs has become the symbol of the new Apple.

Pitfall: Diversification

One of the most damaging mistakes in creating a Personal Brand is to try to be all things to all people. It is impossible. Even with her endeavors in publishing and television production, Oprah Winfrey still stands for a small set of basic values.

Diversification muddies the waters, creates confusion and weakens a brand's strengths. Human attention is a laser beam: tightly focused, it shines intensely on one small area, giving off light and heat. But spread it over a wide area and it becomes diffuse and ineffective. Similarly, a brand that asks its audience to focus its attention too widely fatally weakens that attention. Example: for two decades Kenny Rogers was one of the top-selling country singers. Then he began appearing in television movies and opening roasted chicken restaurants branded with his name. Is Kenny Rogers a country singer or fried chicken pitchman? If you have to ask, he's made a mistake.

Diversification is tempting. It is normal to want to sell to the widest audience possible. It seems logical. But that impulse is a trap. Trying to be the solution to every problem results in a watered down Personal Brand message and overextended resources. Worst of all, it plants seeds of doubt: "If he does so many different things, he can't be very good at any of them."

Specialization implies expertise. Growing a healthy Personal Brand requires choosing a precisely defined *niche* and building your brand around traits that appeal to that niche.

The Process of Specialization

Specialization is a powerful marketing concept. It requires carving out an audience for your marketing from a more general group, then delivering messages specifically crafted to appeal to that audience's needs and concerns. There are four steps to specialization:

1. **Choose your domain:** Should the Personal Brand be aimed at everyone in a profession, or a select subset? You probably already have a good idea, but one of the best ways to narrow things down is to look at segments of the domain that are under-served. For example, instead of marketing to the entire advertising industry, a freelance writer seeking work would market only to graphic design shops, assuming an unmet need for reliable writing.

2. **Know your audience and their needs:** Once you choose your domain, get to know it inside and out:

   a. Its size (number of people)

   b. Its dominant values

   c. Its leadership structure

   d. Its culture (rap, Christian, corporate, etc.)

   e. Its centers of influence (executives, publications, etc.)

   f. The competition

   Talk to people in the domain and discover what the needs are. Often, a domain will have needs you would not expect: leadership, candor in the face of political correctness, humor and irreverence.

3. **Position the brand to meet those needs:** Finally, position the focus of the Personal Brand (attribute or specialty) to appeal to the needs

of the audience. For example, a corporate headhunter focuses his Personal Brand around his array of top-level contacts—an attribute. His domain, entertainment, is notorious for phony promises. So he positions his Personal Brand as "the guy who can get a meeting with anybody," and every week has a new voice mail greeting recorded by one of his well-known pals in the business. This suggests that he meets a need no one else can.

How to Specialize*

There are seven basic ways to specialize a Personal Brand to target a domain:

1. **Specialize by ability:** Build a Personal Brand on having greater ability or showing better results than the competition. Such claims are difficult to support, and people often reject them as hype. But if awards, weighty testimonials or other documented proof of superiority are part of the Brand, it is a powerful differentiator.

2. **Specialize by behavior:** Build a brand identity around personality, manner of speaking, great leadership skills, the ability to listen—any dominant behavior that appeals to your domain and produces a positive reaction.

3. **Specialize by lifestyle:** Living at the beach, traveling the world, driving a vintage Packard, singing in a punk rock band—any aspect of a person's lifestyle that appeals to his domain can be used to specialize.

4. **Specialize by mission:** A Personal Brand can be built around the objectives of the person behind it, whether the goal is to cure a form of cancer, raise money for a new community center, or invent a groundbreaking software product.

---

*Specialization may be the most difficult challenge in creating your Personal Brand. For more help in specialization, visit www.petermontoya.com or call (866) 288-9300.

5. **Specialize by product:** Position the brand as a specialist in a limited, but essential product or line of products. Such extras as fast delivery, wide selection or a guarantee further enhance this specialization.

6. **Specialize by profession:** This is the most basic specialization, ideal for service professionals. It means identifying a niche within a profession and "owning" it via promotion and Personal Brand development. For example, being an ophthalmologic surgeon is not specialization; specializing in laser vision correction for seniors is.

7. **Specialize by service:** Similar to product specialization, this is about narrowing down a wide range of service offerings to the one that is most compelling for the target domain. A freelance writer might choose to specialize in corporate slogans, while an ad agency marketing a Northern California builder might position it as a specialist in environmentally-friendly retail centers.

Barbara Walters built her brand by focusing her efforts towards great interviews and is only approached by Mike Wallace of *60 Minutes*. But where Wallace's Personal Brand is that of the muckraker, Walters' is the gentle surgeon who gets the famous and infamous to open up like no one else can. From her groundbreaking interview with Prime Minister Menachem Begin of Israel and President Anwar Sadat of Egypt in 1977, to her controversial chat with Monica Lewinsky in 1999, Walters has remained relevant, journalistically adept and infinitely skilled.

Pitfall: Dilution

Resist the temptation to dilute a brand by widening its focus, under the misguided impression that it can be leveraged to appeal to a wider audience.

A good example of the failure of this approach is Eddie Murphy. In his post-*Saturday Night Live* days, when he was starring in films like *Trading Places* and touring the country as a standup comedian, Murphy was red-hot. His Personal Brand was the edgy, racially charged black comedian who would say anything to provoke a reaction. Unfortunately, Murphy caught the family entertainment virus and made films like *Dr. Doolittle*. The result? He's disappearing from Hollywood's radar.

Leave a Personal Brand alone once it is established and working. It is critical to retain the tight, stubborn focus that made the brand a success. Change that formula and 99 percent of the time you will drain the energy that makes the brand unique and compelling.

Obeying the Law of Specialization

1. **Select one way to specialize:** Specialize by service, behavior—whatever method suits your Personal Brand and goals. However, only choose after considerable research into your domain. Pay particular attention to competition; try to build your brand on a specialty that is not overcrowded. And be watchful for *unintended specialization*, in which people develop a strong perception of a Personal Brand based on a random incident or characteristic you are not even aware of.

2. **Find a void and fill it:** Locating the under-served areas of an industry or audience is a powerful way to get an advantage on the competition. Example: Author Robert Bly saw an unfilled need in the 1980s of men seeking a path back to traditional masculine values after a decade of "sensitivity." His book, *Iron John*, filled this void and turned Bly into a guru.

3. **Create something new:** Far-fetched? Tell that to the people who created new Internet industries. If there is no void to fill, develop a

Personal Brand that offers a novel product, service or benefit. This can be risky if there is no demand for what you create. But if it works, you will have first-mover advantage. If you are stumped for something new, look at what the competition is doing and do exactly the opposite.

4. **Focus:** When all pieces are in place, hone a Personal Brand like a sharp knife. Instead of constantly doing more, do less. Direct your promotional energies and performance to the single specialization the brand is built around, ignoring opportunities to diversify. Such single-minded dedication increases awareness of a brand's strengths and the perceived value of what is being offered.

Personal Brand Profile

Charles Schwab
Everyman's Investment Advisor

The man whose name is synonymous with discount financial services knew from the beginning that he hated sales. As a teenager, he discovered he had a passion for investing, but as he learned more about the brokerage business, he came to disdain broker commissions and the gouging that often took place. His determination to create a "better way" has made him a household name to millions of ordinary investors.

Charles Schwab [1937 –   ]

Born in Sacramento in 1937, Schwab started his entrepreneurial life selling walnuts—not common black walnuts, but rarer English walnuts that went for a higher price.

At twelve, he switched to collecting and selling eggs, and within a year was selling the chickens as fryers and mixing their droppings with straw to make fertilizer for local gardeners. But it was labor-intensive and time-consuming, so he recreated himself as a golf caddy. Here, he learned that the better the job he did, the bigger the tip.

After graduating from Stanford University in 1959 with a B.A. in Economics, and earning an M.B.A. from Stanford's Graduate School of Business in 1961, Schwab entered the financial services industry. In 1971, he started his San Francisco-based firm as a traditional brokerage company, but in 1974 became a pioneer in the discount brokerage business.

How This Brand Was Built

Schwab built his Personal Brand largely on the audacity of being first. He bought out the partners in his traditional brokerage in 1971, but the watershed moment came when the Securities and Exchange Commission declared a trial period for the deregulation of fixed commissions. Schwab envisioned a discount brokerage that would empower individual investors and provide them with ethical service at a reasonable fee. These were revolutionary concepts in the arcane world of investing, and they quickly made Charles Schwab & Co. a huge success.

Schwab's Personal Brand has also grown in a fertile soil of directness and plain language—personal traits that are reflected in how he runs his vast company. He has nurtured an image of respect for and kinship with the "little guy" investor that has set the direction for his company. Truly, Schwab *is* the company.

Why This Brand Works

- **Authenticity:** Those who know Schwab say his ethics and insistence on financial responsibility are completely genuine. His personal values drive the company's corporate culture and have withstood years of scrutiny.

- **Passion:** In an age when many stockbrokers were flirting with ethical limits to rake in big bucks, Schwab had a mission. "I have a passion for the investor," he says. "I've always been one myself, and the standard I apply is…if it's good for me as an investor, you'll see it."

- **Vision:** Schwab defied the conventions of a multi-billion dollar financial industry in creating a discount brokerage where there were no analysts and all procedures were out front for the consumer to see. In this way, he has built incredible *brand loyalty* for himself and his firm.

Adherence to the Eight Laws

1. **The Law of Specialization.** Schwab saw an under-served need and filled it with his vision and knowledge of his market.

2. **The Law of Leadership.** He is perceived as a pioneer and the man behind the ethical, innovative brokerage that dominates the industry.

3. **The Law of Personality.** Schwab is well-known for his plainspoken, no-nonsense manner and his lack of sales hype, which endears him to his audience.

4. **The Law of Distinctiveness.** The man sometimes gets lost in the glow of Charles Schwab & Co., but he remains unique in his stance as the advocate for the small investor.

5. **The Law of Visibility.** His name has been on the door since Day One.

6. **The Law of Unity.** The integrity and dedication to ethical service publicly espoused by his company are completely in tune with the private Charles Schwab.

7. **The Law of Persistence.** He has grown the discount brokerage—and his Personal Brand—to iconic status in the face of derision, doubt and recession.

8. **The Law of Goodwill.** Schwab is perceived by consumers as their "friend in the business," running the only major brokerage that has *their* interests in mind.

Influence in its Domain

Schwab's vision challenged financial industry practices that suggested the only way to be profitable was to screw the little guy. Then his success shot holes in those notions. His absolute belief in ethical, consumer-centered financial services changed the industry and empowered a generation of investors.

CHAPTER FIVE

Law Two: The Law of Leadership

The source of a great Personal Brand must be recognized as one of the most knowledgeable, respected or skilled in his or her field.

The impulse to follow authority is a remnant of the reptilian brains we inherited from our dinosaur ancestors. Although we have evolved since our *Quest for Fire* days, we still have a hard time resisting authority. In a famous experiment carried out at Yale University, test subjects were instructed to deliver electric shocks to people by pressing a button (the shock "victims" were actually actors pretending to be electrocuted). Even when they believed they were administering dangerous shocks, few test subjects refused to press the button when the scientists told them to. Their instinct was to follow authority, even in defiance of their moral code.

The type of authority we are discussing is less dramatic, but its effect is critical to Personal Brand development. One of the most oft-overlooked facts about Personal Brands is this: *people want to be influenced.* They are looking for someone to cut through uncertainty and hyperbole and offer them a clear path, a product or service that performs as advertised. When a Personal Brand satisfies that impulse, it has real credibility.

Building Authority and Credibility

The Law of Leadership dictates that endowing a Personal Brand with authority and credibility demands that the source be perceived as a leader by the people in his domain. Leadership stems from one of the following:

- **Excellence:** The person is seen as an expert in a certain field, highly experienced, supremely talented, surpassingly intelligent or as someone proven to get results. Performance plays a big part.

- **Position:** The person occupies a position of importance and implied authority, ranging from the head of a union to a board-certified neurologist to a senior vice president.

- **Recognition:** The person has received honors, plaudits and praise from the leaders in his domain: merit awards, media coverage, testimonials, recognition by figures of distinction.

Rather than hype or favoritism, leadership is based on what you know or what you can deliver, and how those things benefit your domain. A great Personal Brand establishes the source as a leader in some way, but it's not necessary to be number one in a field. Being seen as one of the elite in a domain—a top engineer, a savvy corporate lawyer, a brilliant entrepreneur—will do. Mozart may have been the reigning musical genius of his era, but there were others— Haydn and Handel stand out—who are also regarded as masters.*

However, no Personal Brand can afford to be perceived as mediocre. As with Mozart's rival in Peter Shaffer's play *Amadeus*, the bitter composer Salieri, mediocrity does not motivate or build credibility…it simply leads to being forgotten.

---

*What have you mastered? Share your Personal Branding success with me by e-mailing personalbranding@petermontoya.com Your story may be used in my monthly publication, *Personal Branding*.

THE THREE PATHS TO LEADERSHIP

Path One: Excellence

This is the path with the most potential. Followed diligently, it can lead to strong, positive perceptions based on the most precious currency in any profession: *delivering what you promise.* But it is also fraught with peril. Once you establish yourself as one of the elite, you've got to continue to perform at your peak because the expectation is that you will. Drop the ball and you shatter carefully built perceptions.

The Law does not demand that a person be among the elite in every area, but in only one desirable area:

• Talent

• Knowledge and/or education

• Experience

• Proven performance and results

• Effort and work ethic

• Speed

• Sound judgment

• Professionalism

Talent can be outshone by less glamorous characteristics. A gifted but erratic actor may get more work at first than an actor who is moderately talented, hard-working and professional. But eventually word gets out: the gifted flake finds himself struggling while the pro is busy twenty-four seven.

How to Build Leadership by Excellence

- **Narrow it down:** In any domain, there is already someone who is perceived as "the best." So, before Personal Brand development begins, deconstruct your profession or field of expertise and find a specialty at which you excel.

- **Under-promise, over-deliver:** Big claims lead to bigger expectations and enormous disappointments. Instead of promising the moon, under-promise by agreeing to do the expected in the expected time, while planning to deliver more than expected in a shorter time. This grows a Personal Brand that gleams with goodwill.

- **Encourage word of mouth:** Results speak louder than anything. Do great work, make sure people at points of influence know about it, and let the word spread. Nothing is stronger than an unsolicited endorsement.

Pitfall: Over-Promising

One of the quickest ways to turn a Personal Brand into a train wreck is to promise more than you can deliver. People will forgive humble failure, but they will crucify someone who boasts and cannot back it up.

Ex-Seattle Seahawks linebacker Brian Bosworth's extreme "The Boz" persona carried him into the NFL on a wave of braggadocio and obnoxious hype. Unfortunately, he couldn't play, and the only thing he is remembered for is being steamrolled by Bo Jackson on *Monday Night Football*.

Path Two: Position

You can't simply walk into a company and assume the CEO's chair. But building Personal Brand leadership on position doesn't require a person to be at the top, just in a position that has an aura of respect, moral authority, or responsibility. Simply holding such a position enhances a Personal Brand's prestige and credibility.

Of course, there's the matter of *getting* the position in the first place. Some, like CEO or governor, are realistically out of reach. But others may simply take effort and commitment:

- Union leadership

- Board of a professional organization

- Member of a watchdog group

- City council

- Church leadership

- Published columnist

- Member of an awards council

- Member of an activist organization

- Part of a corporate task force

How to Build Leadership by Position

1. **Take action:** Landing a position of influence gets you to the fifty-yard line, but to score, you've got to use the position to effect positive change. The world loathes a do-nothing leader; witness the near-universal contempt for senators whose only interest is getting re-elected. Taking action from a bully pulpit is also one of the best ways to be noticed.

2. **Know your ambition:** Some people don't want the headaches and commitments that come with being head of a corporation or a union, so it is important to know how far you want to rise in an organization before you take a position. Unless advancement and

power serve a Personal Brand's goals, effort is better spent on performance.

3. **Publicize:** A position of importance should not be a secret. Any budding Personal Brand will benefit if people know the person behind the brand is a leader in their domain. Keep it low-key: letterhead, the occasional article, speaking engagements, etc.

Pitfall: Misusing Your Position

Lord Acton's quote, "Power corrupts, and absolute power corrupts absolutely," has proven true on countless occasions. But, a person need not go to extremes to destroy his Personal Brand—apathy, incompetence or greed will do that. You must do more than simply occupy a position, or you risk losing it.

Once former Russian president Boris Yeltsin succeeded Mikhail Gorbachev as the leader of the world's second most powerful nation, his reign boiled down to a series of alcohol-related health disasters and botched decisions involving troops in Chechnya. Eventually, he became a dissipated laughingstock.

Path Three: Recognition

Recognition is a validation of someone's opinion of a Personal Brand—and the human behind it. An award or a citation touches the natural human tendency to go with the crowd, making it "safe" for individuals to hold a high opinion of a person, because others do, too.

Recognition usually goes hand in hand with high achievement, but not always. The critical factor is being recognized for some positive contribution by a source whose opinion your domain respects. Such recognition can come from many sources:

- Industry awards

- Peer awards for quality of work

- Corporate awards

- Publication awards

- Published articles of thanks or reader letters

- Citation for contributions to community or cause

- Lifetime achievement awards

How to Build Leadership by Recognition

1. **Let them know you exist:** An enormous amount of great advertising work goes unrewarded because the awards bodies never know about it. People are usually far too busy working to worry about sending in entry forms. Getting the attention of peers, awards organizations and industry publications is vital.

2. **Know the awards to pursue:** It may not be in your brand's best interest to pursue an award from Greenpeace if your domain consists of conservative Republicans. Research the awards, causes and periodicals and know which ones to pursue.

3. **Publicize:** Once you get the kudos, crow about it. Recognition, whether it is a great review or a "Best of Show" award, is money in the bank. Make it public using the press, personal announcements, statements on stationery and more.

Pitfall: Resting on Laurels

Recognition is not a destination, but simply one more tool to make a Personal Brand more influential. If you forget that and become too satisfied with an award or review, you risk complacency and failure. Stay hungry, even if you're celebrating inside.

After *Star Wars*, George Lucas was on top of the world. Then he let his talents go fallow. He produced and developed special effects and built Lucasfilm—everything but write and direct. When he finally did both in 1999 with *The Phantom Menace*, he had lost a creative step, as the critical barbs attested. His Personal Brand took a beating.

Obeying the Law of Leadership

1. **Choose an area where you already excel:** This gives you an edge and makes work more enjoyable. If there is a lot of competition in your domain with the same skill, find other ways to differentiate.

2. **Hone your skills:** Great athletes become great not because of talent (a dreadfully cheap commodity), but through tireless work. Work to refine your core skill, whether it is a sales pitch, cold read technique or proposal writing. Once you establish yourself as a leader, you must continue to perform at a high level.

3. **Form alliances:** Stand near a bright light and you're illuminated. When recognition is hard to come by—and it often is when a Personal Brand is getting started—it helps to associate with those who are already perceived as leaders.

Personal Brand Profile

Michael Jordan
The Greatest Basketball Player Ever

Jordan is one of the most important African-American Personal Brands in history, one of those rare individuals known simply by his first name. For an entire generation, Jordan embodies a host of perfect virtues: performance under pressure, will to win, perseverance through hardships and passionate pursuit of one's dreams.

Michael Jordan (1963 –   )

Born in 1963 in Brooklyn, Jordan soon moved with his family to Wilmington, North Carolina—a move that foreshadowed the Tar Heel State's influence on his development. As a child, his preferred sport was baseball, but after he began spending a lot of time on the basketball court, his outlook changed.

Ironically, in 1978, when Jordan attended Laney High School in Wilmington, he was cut from the varsity team. But between his sophomore and junior year, Jordan grew from 5'11" to 6'3", and because he had improved greatly as a player, he made varsity the following year.

By the end of his senior year, Jordan had grown to 6'5" and earned a basketball scholarship from the University of North Carolina. There, legendary coach Dean Smith would instill the competitiveness and work ethic that would mark Jordan's rise to NBA greatness.

How This Brand Was Built

Jordan is regarded as the greatest professional basketball player ever to lace up a pair of sneakers—perhaps the greatest athlete of the century. His record of six world championships while dominating the NBA's individual statistics is unparalleled. His ability to achieve peak performance in high-pressure situations and his willingness to "put his team on his back" to carry them to victory made him a superstar like no other.

Off the court, Jordan has been smart, poignant and wildly charismatic. He retired from the NBA in 1994 to pursue his dream of becoming a professional baseball player. When that proved beyond his ability, he returned to the Chicago Bulls and won two more championships. At the same time, he maintained high visibility with a flotilla of endorsements that suited his winning personality and his wholesome image.

In staging another comeback in 2001, Jordan took on another role: elder statesman with something to prove.

Finally, Jordan showed his deeply human side after the murder of his father, James, in 1993.

Why This Brand Works

1. **Excellence:** Leadership is too weak a word. To most knowledgeable people, Jordan was simply "The Best." His reputation was built on one brilliant clutch performance after another...and, at least before his 2001 comeback, he went out on top. His image of excellence is so pervasive that calling someone "the Michael Jordan of..." is shorthand for praising someone at the pinnacle of his abilities.

2. **Universality:** He is one of the few athletes with absolutely universal appeal—for men, women, white, black, old, and young.

3. **Values:** More than any other major public figure of the last twenty-five years, Jordan epitomizes the values we cherish as Americans: perseverance, unbreakable will, good humor, intelligence, humanity and the ceaseless drive to excel.

4. **Involvement:** Jordan hardly faded from the scene since his retirement. He surfaced as co-owner and general manager of the Washington Wizards, co-owner of a pro hockey team, commercial spokesman...and then he started at small forward for the Wizards in the 2001 – 2002 NBA season.

Adherence to the Eight Laws

1. **The Law of Specialization.** There is only one Michael Jordan—a player who combines athletic grace, skill, will to win, competitive fire and charisma in a way no athlete has since Muhammad Ali.

2. **The Law of Leadership.** No player in the history of pro basketball has as thoroughly dominated the game, both from an individual and team perspective.

3. **The Law of Personality**. Jordan's driven, yet ebullient personality comes through both on and off the court in his roles as ruthless opponent-killer and product pitchman.

4. **The Law of Distinctiveness.** Jordan rose above the anonymity of being just another basketball player to become the standard by which all other players are judged: "That play was Jordanesque!"

5. **The Law of Visibility.** Jordan's face was the face of the NBA earlier in his career, and during his comeback he remains the sport's most compelling personality.

6. **The Law of Unity.** Jordan's private life had its ups and downs, taking a few knocks over allegations of major gambling debts. But overall, Jordan the player and Jordan the family man seem to fit together seamlessly.

7. **The Law of Persistence.** Jordan has never lost the trait that symbolized him most: his ferocious drive to be the best. Even his ill-fated stint as a minor leaguer was seen as the action of a great man trying to conquer a new challenge. Even his comeback, fraught as it is with the risk that he will tarnish his legacy, represents his unquenchable fire.

8. **The Law of Goodwill.** Except for some die-hard fans in New York, Cleveland, Miami, Detroit...Jordan was and is regarded with almost universal admiration.

Influence in Its Domain

Michael Jordan catapulted the NBA from the Magic Johnson-Larry Bird era into a new age of primetime television, big ratings and great playoff rivalries. As the perfect spokesman—charming, virtuous and extraordinarily gifted—he became the league's global face, and must be considered a major factor behind basketball's mushrooming worldwide popularity.

CHAPTER SIX

Law Three: The Law of Personality

A great Personal Brand is built around the source's personality in all its aspects, including its flaws.

Americans take inordinate delight in the misfortunes of the powerful, the arrogant and those who radiate perfection. We love a karmic comeuppance. With that fact in mind, it is perplexing that so many public figures persist in trying to create images that paint them as flawless pillars of virtue, faith and family. This points to blatant ignorance of a simple truth: we like people who are "real," and we are willing to forgive a lot if a person simply lets himself be human like the rest of us.

You Are Your Product

The Law of Personality states that a great Personal Brand must be built on a foundation of the source's true personality*, flaws and all. At the core of any successful brand lies a real person, not a public relations-crafted Frankenstein's monster. It is a law that removes some of the pressure laid on by the Law of Leadership: you've got to be good, but you don't have to be *perfect*.

---

*Share how your personality helped you climb the success ladder. Your story may be used in my monthly publication. E-mail me at personalbranding@petermontoya.com.

Filling a Psychological Need

Great Personal Brands fill psychological needs in their domains—for creativity, candor, compassion, leadership and so on. The product, service or behavior that fills that need should be superior.

But outside of professional performance, humans need to feel equal to the best and the brightest. So not only is it fine for a brilliant attorney to go out with her clients after a big case, have a few drinks and showcase a taste for dirty jokes, it is even beneficial—a reminder that brilliant or not, she is as human as the rest of us. This law reminds us that creating and maintaining a Personal Brand is inextricably bound up with issues of ego.

The Four Personality Traits

Freud be damned, these are the four aspects that must be gauged and managed to build an effective Personal Brand—especially if you are a public relations professional or publicist managing a highly visible person:

1. **Relatability**

2. **Fallibility**

3. **Positivism**

4. **Authenticity**

A Personal Brand doesn't have to project all four to be successful; two of them will do in most cases. But it is important that all four be identified and the ones that aren't strengths be dealt with in a non-damaging way.

Key Personality Trait: Relatability

Call it the Knowing Nod Effect. You see it all the time at standup comedy shows when the comedian reels off a joke that sends the audience into gales of laughter, with half of them nodding knowingly: "Yes, I know exactly what you're talking about. I've done it, too."

Relatability in a Personal Brand lets others identify with the source, finding a common intellectual, emotional or moral ground on which they can meet and do business.

With a relatable Personal Brand, people in the domain see something of themselves reflected in the brand. It could be something as trifling as a style of dress or as profound as a shared religious conviction. In any case, recognition translates into connection and comfort with the Personal Brand, before the source even appears on the scene.

Rosie O'Donnell and Helen Hunt have benefited hugely from their ability to evoke feelings of commonality, warmth and empathy. O'Donnell has done so by being overweight, brash, motherly, politically incorrect, emotional—everything most polished celebrities are not. Women look at her and see the funny, loud girl they grew up with. Hunt has become Hollywood's beauty next door, a non-glamorous, self-deprecating "Everywoman". Even to most women, she is utterly non-threatening.

Using Relatability

1. **If you don't have it, don't try to get it:** Relatability is like a great throwing arm: if you weren't born with it, it's tough to develop. Don't try—you'll appear artificial and forced.

2. **Be yourself:** You won't connect with everyone, so don't attempt to. Watering down your personality will only prevent anyone from identifying with you.

3. **Emphasize personality traits:** If you believe your domain will relate to aspects of your personality, emphasize them in your brand development.

4. **Research:** If people of influence in your domain aren't relating to you, learn more about them—their interests, their background, etc. You might find something you already have in common. Then it's just a matter of bringing it to their attention.

Pitfall: Remoteness

In his 1996 bid for the presidency, Bob Dole was the picture of the remote, out-of-touch white male Republican. Despite poll numbers that showed him heading for a political Waterloo, he trudged along his Personal Brand path: the stolid war veteran who stood for the American family values Bill Clinton seemed to mock.

It was no contest. What made Dole's resounding defeat a shame was that underneath the mortician exterior, Dole is a *funny* guy. Since then he has done commercials, Leno, Letterman and so on, showing a hip sense of humor and a gift for gentle self-parody that are admirable in any politician. But in his campaign, none of it came out.

Key Personality Trait: Fallibility

The cover-up *always* hurts more than the crime. Ask Nixon. You'd think politicians would learn, but obfuscation seems as human as procreation. The fact is, Americans love to forgive, and to a person who admits his failure and accepts responsibility, we're the soul of absolution.

Smart Personal Brand development doesn't broadcast a person's flaws and foibles, but it doesn't deny them. Since everyone has their warts, letting flaws show once in a while puts people at ease and enhances relatability. In addition, some flaws are "expected" in certain professions: organizational fussiness in an engineer, a temper in an artist, glibness in a salesman and so on. Such flaws can render the brand picture even clearer.

Five Tips for Positively Spinning Flaws

1. **Admission:** Admit the short temper, the big ego, the impatience, the problem with punctuality.

2. **Humor:** Don't take yourself too seriously. Own up to the flaw with an "Yeah, I know I'm a jerk" attitude, which suggests awareness of the problem and the willingness to be kidded about it.

3. **Benefit:** Point out how the flaw can actually be a good thing. For example, a foul mouth could be spun as a sign of the passion you bring to your work.

4. **Control:** Finally, control the bad temper or the caffeine habit or the tendency to gossip. No matter how it's spun, an uncorrected flaw will wear thin.

5. **Timing:** Address flaws or a questionable history early. "Seedy stuff in the past can be spun to benefit your brand before it's big," says Harvard's Fournier, "but when your brand is big, it can be hugely negative and needs active management."

Drew Barrymore is an example of the redemptive power of spinning your flaws. A precious child star in *E.T.*, she became enamored of alcohol and drugs in her pre-teen years, spiraling into a life of abuse, tantrums and a dying career. Barrymore began to turn the tide with an autobiography, *Little Girl Lost*, in which she spoke candidly about her addictions, her behavior and her responsibility for her choices. A series of well-received performances in films like *Boys on the Side* and *Scream* showed that thanks to her honesty and sense of humor about her problems, audiences had not only forgiven her, they had embraced her.

Pitfall: Arrogance

We *love* to watch an arrogant man go down. Microsoft Chairman Bill Gates is many things, but humble is not one of them. At this writing, it was unclear where the federal government's antitrust action against Microsoft would end up, but the fact remains that Gates was devastating to his company's chances because of his arrogant, dismissive attitude in a videotaped deposition. Dan Goodin, in his November 16, 1998 story for *News.com*, wrote, "At points in this morning's proceedings, the deposition seemed to amuse just about everyone in the courtroom, with United States District Judge Thomas Penfield Jackson as well as Microsoft lawyers laughing at the squabbling between Gates and his interviewers." Observers claimed that Gates had long believed that no one could touch Microsoft—that it was, in effect, above the law. That prevailing attitude may still lead to a costly setback for the world's biggest software maker.

Key Personality Trait: Positivism

Step into a crowded room and you notice it: people create energy. It can either elevate everyone or bring everyone down. And nothing sucks the energy from a situation like negative thinking.

Positivism does not mean being an officious, saccharine cheerleader; such people provoke violence in the mildest-mannered. It simply means building one or more of the following qualities into a Personal Brand:

• Perseverance against odds

• Enthusiasm

• Praise and encouragement of others

- The ability to extract a benefit from a defeat

- Accommodation

A positive Personal Brand creates the perception that its source consistently sees the glass as half-full, suffusing it with a "find a way to get it done" aura that is priceless.

Lance Armstrong: Hero

If anyone is an example of the transcendent power of positive thinking and perseverance, it is Lance Armstrong. In 1996, as he was ascending the world cycling ranks, Armstrong was diagnosed with testicular cancer. Worse yet, the tumors had spread to his abdomen, lungs, lymph nodes and brain. Armstrong was given a 40 percent chance of survival. His French cycling team cut him, and the cycling world wrote him off. But Armstrong maintained that he was going to race competitively again, though few gave him any chance. But in 1999, after winning several preliminary races, he tackled and won the Tour de France—and to prove his victory was not a fluke, repeated in 2000 and 2001. Today, Armstrong stands as extraordinary testament to the power of belief and refusal to surrender.

Pitfall: Pessimism

I tried to think of a notable Personal Brand that had met its downfall due to pessimism, but there aren't any. That is the lesson here: negative, defeatist thinking is cancer to a Personal Brand. Nothing kills enthusiasm, loyalty, team spirit and a sense of the possible quite like it. It's fine to be coldly realistic, as long as you propose constructive action. But pure pessimism guarantees a place on the professional scrap heap.

Nothing great was ever achieved by a pessimist.

Key Personality Trait: Authenticity

Everything begins with authenticity. It is the fountainhead for relatability and fallibility. Authenticity simply means that whoever you really are, you must let it come out in your Personal Brand. Your true self may be revealed in traits that are highly relatable, or your flaws might show through brightest. Or perhaps you will reveal some idiosyncrasy that is in a category all its own, that makes you unique or memorable. In any case, a Personal Brand built on authenticity feels real and connects with its audience in a way no artificial construct, carefully built on focus groups and market research, can.

Explain It Early, Explain It Honestly and Explain It Yourself

In an age of spin, people respect the unvarnished truth. No one wants to feel manipulated. Remember this axiom: *who you really are will come out.* So "out" yourself. Instead of hiding your oddities and eccentricities, weave them into your Personal Brand, so that they seem part of the entire package. If they are discovered against your will, people will assume what they want, and they may assume you are hiding something. Taking control of that process allows you to be yourself, and that's what it's all about.

60 Minutes correspondent Andy Rooney is a great example of a Personal Brand built on a man being himself, without apology. Rooney is a professional curmudgeon whose rants about the vagaries of modern life are part commentary, part whine. If you were grooming a journalist to be a celebrity, you'd drink poison before making him like Rooney. He's fussy, picky, and sometimes damned annoying. But he's real, and so are many of his insights. People respect the fact that Rooney hasn't tried to polish his persona to make himself appealing to the largest possible audience. Quite the contrary. He is who he is, and we embrace him for being as odd as the rest of us.

Pitfall: Phoniness

There are two ways to fake a Personal Brand: copy someone else or fabricate one out of thin air. Duplication is the venial sin of the two; Anna Nicole Smith became an object of derision in her desire to be the next Marilyn Monroe, but at least she is still working.

Fabrication, on the other hand, is a one-way ticket to Hell. For example, the singing duo Milli Vanilli, who won the Best New Artist Grammy in 1989 for their album *Girl You Know It's True.* Unfortunately for them, Rob Pilatus and Fab Morvan were revealed to be impostors, hired by German producer Frank Farian to lip synch music created by others as part of a musical "concept." This, combined with the pair's arrogant statements that they would be "bigger than the Beatles," earned them blistering humiliation from fans and music pros. More than a decade later they are still infamous.

Obeying the Law of Personality

measure self on 4 Traits

- **Measure for the Four Traits:** The first step is to measure that brand for relatability, fallibility, positivism and authenticity. Rate each on a 1 – 10 scale and you'll know which areas to emphasize and which to play down.

- **Turn weaknesses into strengths:** Traits that rate below 5 are potential problems, but they can be managed. For instance, a person who is naturally aloof with others rates low on the relatability scale. Rather than positioning that person against type as friendly and charming, manage expectations by creating a Personal Brand that emphasizes professionalism and a down-to-business demeanor.

- **Be obvious:** People cannot hide who they are, so go in the opposite direction and celebrate your personality in all its forms. Dress to suit it, design business cards to suit it and so on. Broadcasting lets you manage first impressions.

- **Adjust:** Remain aware of how the personality behind a Personal Brand is affecting its domain. If you suspect it is not a good fit, watch for warning signs: sudden changes in goodwill, reluctance to introduce the person to superiors, etc. Be aware and be able to change the personality traits you emphasize, or change domains.

Personal Brand Profile

Oprah Winfrey
Crusader for Women's Empowerment

There is little doubt that the respect and admiration with which Oprah Winfrey is regarded would make her a leading presidential candidate if she ever ran. Unquestionably the most influential African-American woman in the world, she has a Personal Brand that stands out for its power, its pervasiveness and its humanity.

Oprah Winfrey (1954 –   )

Winfrey was born in Kosciusko, Mississippi in 1954, and raised by her paternal grandmother until age six. After going to live with her mother in Milwaukee, her childhood became troubled, including sexual abuse at the hands of male relatives. At age thirteen, she went to live with her father in Nashville. Here, she began to excel in school, winning a full scholarship to Tennessee State University.

While still in school she became the first African-American woman to anchor a newscast in Nashville. After graduation, she moved to Baltimore to work as a reporter and co-anchor for WJZ-TV. A year later she became co-host of the station's morning show, *People Are Talking*. From there she moved to Chicago to become host of *A.M. Chicago*. Within three months, her ratings surpassed Phil

Donahue's, and a year later the show went national and was renamed *The Oprah Winfrey Show*.

How This Brand Was Built

Winfrey is a multimedia tycoon, producing film and television programs, and, by 2000, was launching her own magazine, *O: The Oprah Magazine*, the most successful magazine start-up in history. Everything flows from her talk show, which she has used as a platform for sharing her struggles with sexual abuse and her weight. Most importantly, Winfrey has used the show to build a deep, personal connection with her audience, most of whom feel her values and aspirations reflect theirs.

Winfrey has also built her Personal Brand around her desire to build, produce and promote worthwhile projects. Her *Oprah's Book Club* has become a marketing force in the publishing industry, providing an audience for out-of-the-mainstream authors who might otherwise have languished on the bookshelves. In building an empire, she has become admired as an example of what a woman can do if she sets her mind to it.

Why This Brand Works

- **Honesty:** The core of Winfrey's Personal Brand is her openness about herself with her audience. Their genuine love for her stems from the perception that she has revealed herself to them and established an honest connection.

- **Control:** Winfrey is vigorously protective of her privacy, maintaining tight control over information released for public consumption. This not only prevents gossip, it is a manifestation of her drive and ambition.

- **Virtue:** When talk shows were heading toward tabloid exploitation, Winfrey steered hers toward motivation and self-help. This set the tone for her positive Personal Brand.

- **Perseverance:** "Don't be satisfied with just one success—and don't give up after one failure." That attitude has sustained Winfrey through film project failures, a very public personal life and her own weight problems.

Adherence to the Eight Laws

1. **The Law of Specialization.** Though she began as "another talk show host," Winfrey quickly differentiated herself with positivism, ambition and an honest desire to build a legacy of worthwhile work.

2. **The Law of Leadership.** She has made herself a mogul with hard work and vision—a voice of power and control in entertainment, media and publishing.

3. **The Law of Personality.** No celebrity has gained more from openly sharing her struggles, hopes and emotions with her audience.

4. **The Law of Distinctiveness.** She quickly set herself apart from the trailer-trash world of talk show hosts by becoming much more: a positive force, a champion of unknown talent and an outspoken advocate for women.

5. **The Law of Visibility.** How could you improve on having your own talk show and magazine? Oprah is one of the few known only by her first name.

6. **The Law of Unity.** It is hard to gauge this one, because Winfrey guards her privacy so jealously. But since no scandals have emerged, it's safe to assume that the public and private woman are unified.

7. **The Law of Persistence.** She has never wavered from her core persona: flawed, driven, compassionate and always ready with a "you can do it" cheer.

8. **The Law of Goodwill.** It is hard to think of a woman who is loved more intensely and with greater devotion and admiration than Winfrey.

Influence in Its Domain

Oprah Winfrey has changed the landscape of women's media with her magazine, her founding of the Internet and cable network Oxygen Media, and her relentless commitment to positive, productive, empowering works. "I want to be working on projects that are meaningful," she says. "I know that can sound superficial, but it's true. I would like to be able to say, down the road, that I created a legacy, something even more enduring than anything I've done yet."

CHAPTER SEVEN

Law Four: The Law of Distinctiveness

A great Personal Brand only becomes burned onto people's minds if it is expressed in a unique way.

You're flipping channels and you come upon a nature show. In it, a scholarly-looking naturalist is standing by a trussed-up crocodile, talking calmly about its habits and its appetite. You flip further and a hyperactive Australian is wrestling with a fourteen-foot saltwater croc—nearly being devoured, getting covered in mud, and exclaiming things like, "Crikey! Isn't she a beauty!" Which do you watch?

Steve Irwin, otherwise known as the Crocodile Hunter, is a perfect example of distinctive Personal Branding. He has differentiated himself from every other nature show host by being, well, out of his bloody mind. There may be other reptile experts with greater knowledge, but Irwin stands out by being utterly distinctive.

The Law of Distinctiveness states that an effective Personal Brand needs to be expressed in a way that is different from the competition. Once you have followed the Law of Specialization and built a Personal Brand around a unique skill or attribute, developing that brand means projecting it in a unique way. Just as a startlingly different package design makes a product jump off the shelf, distinctiveness does the same for a Personal Brand.

Differentiate or Die

In his book, *The Want Makers: Lifting the Lid off the Advertising Industry*, Eric Clark asserts that the average American will see about 2 million television advertising messages by age sixty-five. Factor in print, radio, outdoor, direct marketing and other sources, and you begin to understand why we have been desensitized. That fact gives you, the brave Personal Brand builder, an advantage.

Promoting a Personal Brand is a considerable investment, whether it's by a huge record company or a self-employed individual. Consequently, most people play it safe: they construct a middle-of-the-road brand that will not offend anyone, then are excruciatingly careful that it does not stand out too much. *This is the route to failure*. Such marketers quickly become risk-averse, ensuring that they and their brand will remain anonymous among the multitudes.

Repel People You Don't Want

Individuals and marketers often make Personal Brands trendy or vanilla to avoid offending anyone. It is the *wrong* instinct. A truly distinctive Personal Brand *should* offend or put off some people—it's desirable! It is impossible to create a great Personal Brand that won't elicit disapproval from a segment of its audience, so don't try. If a group doesn't "get it," the brand is probably sending a vibrant, brazen message to those who will.

Do not let the bafflement of some dissuade you from daring choices; embrace the confusion as proof that your Personal Brand is staking out its own territory. If your brand lacks the energy to repel the people that you don't want, good luck attracting the people you do want.

The Three Areas of Distinction*

1. **Behavior:** This can be anything from the way a person speaks or laughs to the jokes he tells, how he performs and interacts in a team situation or how much emotion he shows.

2. **Physicality:** This is how a person dresses or wears his hair, what kind of jewelry or body piercings he has, what kind of shape he is in or how he walks or carries himself.

3. **Lifestyle:** This encompasses everything from hobbies to religion to politics to social life. This type of distinction is most often reflected in the phrase "He's the _____ who _____ s," as in "He's the surgeon who surfs."

Distinguishing by Behavior

The challenge in building distinction into a Personal Brand based on behavior is recognizing the behavior itself. Most people bear at least one behavioral trait that is normal to them, but would seem unusual and memorable to others. The trick is recognizing that trait, whether for your own brand or as an objective party, determining if it is appropriate for your domain, and then working that trait into the Personal Brand.

For our purposes, behavior falls into four basic groups:

1. **Speech:** Distinction by speech could involve an accent, a catch phrase, an inflection or even speaking very fast or very slowly. Speech styles or patterns are immediately noticeable to those in your domain, and can be communicated without any special effort. Since speech patterns or habits tend to be among the most ingrained behavioral traits, get the help of others to determine what is unique about your speech.

---

*What makes you unique? Share your story at personalbranding@petermontoya.com, and I may use it in my monthly publication, *Personal Branding.*

2. **Humor:** Instead of a style of communication, humor is a way of thinking. Depending on the domain, puns, gallows humor, brain-teasers or Algonquin Round Table-style witticisms might be just the thing for setting you apart from the competition. Obviously, make sure the style of humor—and even the use of humor—is appropriate to the domain.

3. **Process:** Process is the way in which a person approaches his or her work: in an orderly fashion, in chaos, methodically, at the last minute and so on. Process can be worked into a Personal Brand by being consistent and making others aware that "This is how I work." The process must be seen as an integral to your professional DNA.

4. **Effect on others:** Inspiring, relaxing or increasing the tension in others are all manifestations of this type of behavior. Here, a Personal Brand is not set apart by what its source does, but how others react to the source. To fully leverage this, take careful note of how others react to your presence and your process, then bring that reaction to the attention of people of influence. For example, an engineer whose "out of the box" thinking inspires other engineers is an asset.

Pitfall: Behavioral Overkill

You can take a behavioral quirk too far. Speaking so forcefully that others feel like they can't get a word in edgewise, telling offensive jokes, doing 90 percent of the work on a project just before the dead-line—these are all examples of behavior that wears thin very quickly. Rather than enhance a Personal Brand, it can cripple it.

Distinguishing by Physicality

You don't need to wear a long black coat in August or spike your hair into pink Statue of Liberty points to be distinctive by physical attributes; you just need to establish a single physical characteristic that is permanently associated with you. As with behavior, a physical distinguisher should be natural and already worked into the source's life. In making it part of the Personal Brand, you are merely calling the domain's attention to it.

Physicality falls into three basic groups:

- **Clothing:** An easy one. The trick is not only to become known for a certain style of clothing, but to ensure that it is not seen as a trend. For instance, a designer wearing all black was once hip. Now it is passé. Signature clothing could be always wearing beach clothes, always dressing in designer suits, always wearing a hat and so on.

  Note the use of "always." Work your signature apparel into your professional wardrobe at every turn. Think of Johnny Cash, and besides country music, what comes to mind? Black clothes.

- **Body:** There are not many people who want to be known as "the obese attorney." Physically nondescript? Out of luck. But if you're fit, tall, short, walk with a limp...well, you get the picture. Into this category fall characteristics like posture, weight, gait and so on.

  You generally cannot create distinction based on body traits; the people in your domain will do it. But you can make sure the memorable trait is displayed and not hidden.

- **General appearance:** Into this bucket go all the things not covered by clothing and body: teeth, piercings, facial features, hair color and style, you name it. You can exercise greater control over these traits: choosing to die your hair neon green, for example. This control means that, as with clothing, you can design your appearance to suit your domain. However, the same wisdom applies: do not take on affectation to fit into a domain. It will backfire.

  Suit the appearance feature to the domain. I don't recommend tongue piercings for an aspiring corporate speaker.

Pitfall: Artificiality

Going over the top in physicality to draw attention is a certain ticket to being branded a poseur, one who affects the mannerisms of others to win favor. If a type of clothing, hairstyle or jewelry is not already part of who a person is, it should be left alone.

The perfect example of this is Michael Jackson. Once the King of Pop, in recent years he has slid into a kind of pathetic parody continuum, and nothing has fueled the "weirdo" talk more than his remarkably altered appearance.

Distinguishing by Lifestyle

A lifestyle might incorporate aspects of behavior or physicality, but it still stands separate from them as a distinguisher. A lifestyle is anything the source does outside of his domain that has a reflection on his Personal Brand. For example, a security consultant might be an avid competitive sailor in his spare time, and visit a client wearing deck shoes and a deep suntan. In doing so, he is advertising the fact that he is a sailor, complete with all the attendant images.

Lifestyles fall into two basic groups:

1. **Culture:** Alternative, gay, green, scholar…these are some of the dozens of cultural labels people attach to themselves. Culture represents a defined way of living usually associated with a movement, group or viewpoint. Membership in any culture carries with it an expectation of certain behaviors, but whether you follow them is up to you. It is certainly easier to broadcast yourself as an environmental activist if you wear hemp clothing and eat vegan, but you also risk being hit with stereotypes.

2. **Activities:** If you have a consuming hobby, interest or pastime, it can be a distinguisher. Sailing, surfing, acting, singing in a band,

baseball fanaticism, stamp collecting—they're all potential ways to set yourself apart within your domain.

As with culture, activities carry with them some perceptual baggage—people assume if you do something, certain facts must apply to you. For example, if you are a sailor, your baggage may include the perception that you are decisive and love the challenge of taking on nature. Be sure the baggage looks good on you.

Pitfall: Offensive Lifestyle

No one would ever suggest that you abandon a lifestyle choice for fear of what it might do to your career. However, if you engage in a lifestyle that might prove offensive to your domain, be prepared for the consequences.

For example, ex-NBA star Dennis Rodman had built a very hip Personal Brand as a bad boy, gambler and all-around head case when he left pro basketball. But by the time he had become better known for debauched beachfront parties, rape charges and police nuisance calls, his brand had been irreparably polluted. Today, he is largely regarded with contempt and pity.

Running Against the Herd

Being distinctive is hard. And I'm not just talking from the ad agency perspective of finding an original concept with which to brand a client. Finding the courage to buck the system and swim against the current is hard...and frightening. But that's what it takes to build a great Personal Brand.

There are some very real psychological reasons why people are compelled to follow the herd, to not stand out or be noticed. In a 1998 speech to the Investors Research Institute, Dr. Richard Geist, Ph.D., editor of *Strategic Investing* and a professor of social psychology at Harvard University, illustrated several factors defining the micro-cap stock investor that, coincidentally, also form the core of the herd mentality:

- **Sense of mirroring:** The person's judgments and creativity are validated, which leads to growth and development. To have a sense of mirroring, human beings need feedback and to feel appreciated.

- **Idealizing:** The person likes the idea of being part of something larger than himself. It conveys power and knowledge.

- **Partnering:** The person enjoys having a sense of sameness, identifying with like-minded others, and sharing beliefs and tools.

The surrounding culture exerts pressure to conform by positively rewarding those who do with a sense of validating their own choices. At the same time, it sanctions those who refuse to conform by expressing confusion or disdain—withholding that all-important tacit approval. Creating a great Personal Brand requires the willingness to defy the herd—and a confidence bordering on arrogance.

Obeying the Law of Distinctiveness

- **Do a one-eighty on the competition:** Look at the competition and learn how they are distinguishing themselves. Then do the opposite. For example: you're a marketing strategist building a Personal Brand for a motivational speaker. You look at the competition and find that they are mostly positioning themselves as positive, "You can do it" cheerleaders. You decide to position your brand the other way: as a sarcastic, wisecracking cynic, based on his wiseguy personality. Will the brand turn some people off? Yes. But it will also stand out.

- **Tie your distinction to what you do:** When possible, connect your distinguishing trait to your profession. There are three ways to do it: as a part of your work, as the way you deal with others, or as a symbol of the spirit behind your work. Your process is a good example of the first; your speech or effect on others is a good example of the second. And almost any lifestyle or cultural choice is an indicator of the third—a surfing lifestyle shows you have a free spirit, etc.

- **Go public:** Make sure the audience knows what the distinguisher is. You can broadcast it overtly, telling them straight out. Or you can show the trait boldly without saying a word. Either way, they'll figure it out. Just cultivate some audacity and let the audience know what makes your brand different.

- **Persist:** As a Personal Brand source, it takes time for the distinctiveness of a brand to percolate down through the consciousness of your audience. Once you find your distinguisher, stick with it. Do not change it; you'll look like a trend whore. Give it time, and if you've chosen it well for your audience, it will have an effect.

Personal Brand Profile

Jimmy Buffett
Margaritas for the Masses

No one embodies the indolent, beach bum, tropical party image of Key West and the Caribbean like Jimmy Buffett, the failed country rocker turned conglomerate. This son of a son of a sailor has turned a genuine passion for the beachcomber life, a talent for writing joyous pop tunes and sparkling ballads, and a savvy for giving his audiences the fantasy they crave into a $50 million empire.

Jimmy Buffett (1946 –   )
Buffett was born in 1946 in Pascogoula, Mississippi, and soon moved with his family to Mobile, Alabama, where his father's job

at the Alabama Dry Docks and Shipyard influenced Buffett's love of the ocean. His grandfather, James Sr., who captained his own ship, Chicamauga, also shaped the young man's view of the sailor's life with his many sea stories.

Buffett took his taste for southern roots music to the University of Southern Mississippi, where he graduated in 1969 with a degree in history and journalism. But the most important development of his time at school was seeing how his roommate, a musician, attracted girls with his guitar playing and singing. Buffett himself picked up the guitar, which would lead to his fateful move to Nashville and the development of his unique, Gulf Coast style.

How This Brand Was Built

Buffett went to Nashville in the late '60s to build his country music career, but his first album was a flop. Moving to Key West, Florida, he showed his smarts by developing the "island-inflected folk pop" and the beach bum persona that would carry him to stardom. After a few hits and strong album sales backed by constant touring, things started to slow in the 1980s. Always a sharp self-promoter, Buffett saw that his fans were treating his music as a symbol of a lifestyle, so he changed his shows to celebrate that lifestyle, in a sort of traveling musical beach party. Today, the ideal of "Margaritaville" has made Buffett's "parrothead" fans among the world's most devoted, and his Personal Brand one of the world's most unique.

Why This Brand Works

1. **Authenticity:** Buffett isn't some corporate creation who poses in front of a Key Largo beach bar and then jets off to a condo in Miami Beach; he's the real McCoy. He has lived the tropical life he writes about—flown the seaplanes, sailed the ocean, met the characters. As a result, he is very real.

2. **Resonance:** The aura of Margaritaville strikes a chord with every overworked computer technician and tired teacher. The idea Buffett promotes, that you can escape to a tropical paradise for awhile in his concerts, is extremely appealing, and it is one of the reasons he inspires such devotion.

3. **Quality:** All the auras in the world wouldn't be enough to sustain his Personal Brand if Buffett didn't write good songs and put on a great show. He does. His writing has always been the strongest part of his creativity, and his stage show, with clowns, dancers, steel drums and more, is a spectacle.

4. **Expansion:** Buffett is a sharp businessman as well as a musician. The hunger for the Margaritaville life led him to open stores selling "parrothead" merchandise, create a Web site and even launch his own brand of tequila.

Adherence to the Eight Laws

1. **The Law of Specialization.** There is no one else in his position, perhaps because to try to horn in on Buffett's territory today would seem utterly artificial.

2. **The Law of Leadership.** Buffett's success has not been built on musical genius, but on his representation of a coveted lifestyle, so he is the leader of the lifestyle.

3. **The Law of Personality.** The man's personality is in every song and in the entire Margaritaville culture. He hides little and seems to adore both his music and his fans.

4. **The Law of Distinctiveness.** He expresses his Personal Brand with music that is, for all intents and purposes, dead in an era of hip-hop and pop. The island flavor of the product and the culture it creates stand out brightly.

5. **The Law of Visibility.** Outside his domain, Buffett is not on the public radar screen, which costs him points. But inside his domain, where it really matters, he is everywhere—like a deity.

6. **The Law of Unity.** Buffett erects no barriers between his audience and himself, and the longevity of his success shows that the public persona and the private man are the same: kindly beach bums with business savvy.

7. **The Law of Persistence.** He has never tried to go hard rock, or back to his country roots. Buffett knows a good thing when he has it, and his formula has not changed.

8. **The Law of Goodwill.** His fans are a barometer: other than Deadheads, no group of fans is more dedicated, more positive or more joyous.

Influence in its Domain

Jimmy Buffett's invitation to "change your latitude" is not part of the bigger cultural landscape. But in his personally created subculture, where college kids and boomers and parents dream of sailing the waters off Antigua, he has a powerful, positive effect. Parrothead Clubs have sprung up all over the United States, working on causes from beach cleanups to fundraising. So, though his overall influence remains compartmentalized, in his domain, his influence is omnipotent.

CHAPTER EIGHT

Law Five: The Law of Visibility

A great Personal Brand must be seen—consistently and repeatedly— by everyone in its domain.

I call it the Fallacy of Apparent Quality, and it is as old as business. A businessman opens a shop that offers the best products at the fairest prices. He and his staff offer expert advice and wonderful service. It's truly a great business—but the owner makes the fatal mistake of assuming that because he knows his shop is fabulous, everyone else will, as if by magic. So he doesn't advertise. Eventually, he folds, still wondering "I built it, why didn't they come?"

Because he didn't *tell* them to come. People don't find out about a quality product—or a Personal Brand—by telepathy; you've got to tell them about it. The Law of Visibility states that to work, a Personal Brand must be seen over and over again, until it imprints itself on the consciousness of its domain. No matter how great a brand is, it's worth zilch if nobody knows about it.

Visibility Matters More than Ability

This is a tough pill for many people to swallow. They refuse to accept that quality means less to the success of a Personal Brand than simply being seen and known. Well, performance is the most important element *after your Personal Brand has become known*. Until then, the most difficult task is getting it known, and that means getting it visible.

Visibility creates the *presumption* of quality. Others assume because they see a person all the time, he must be superior to others offering the same product or service. Visibility creates familiarity, which creates comfort with a buying or hiring decision. Are there actors and martial artists who are better than Chuck Norris? Absolutely. But Norris has stayed in the public eye for so long with *Walker: Texas Ranger*, karate tournaments and infomercials, he has got "top of mind" awareness and a strong Personal Brand.

The Three Paths to Visibility

Getting visible takes work. For the appealing traits of a Personal Brand to become known and permeate the domain, its key message must be broadcast repeatedly, with clockwork regularity. There are three ways to generate visibility:

- Planning

- Leveraging opportunity

- Accident

Visibility Through Planning

This is also known as promotion and marketing. It is the most effective form of visibility: managed—controlled—expected. By advertising a Personal Brand or networking at professional events, you begin to create brand awareness at your own pace. You begin to create the *perception* of being in demand, which ultimately leads to the reality of being in demand.

Planned visibility is one of the must-have components of any successful Personal Brand; without it you are relying on chance opportunity to get the brand known. It takes, as the name suggests, *planning*. Marketing strategies, research, deployment calendars, budgets—they are all part of the visibility offensive.

Arnold Schwarzenegger has kept his eyes on the prize—stardom—since his days as a bodybuilder in Austria. His victory in the 1967 Mr. Universe competition led him to the United States, where he made plans to become a movie star. From the time he landed his first major role in 1982's *Conan the Barbarian*, Schwarzenegger focused his energies and considerable intellect on building his persona as the ultimate action hero...and his status at the top of the Hollywood mountain attests to his success.*

Pitfall: Overexposure

A Personal Brand can be too visible for its own good and have a negative effect. Too much advertising or too many appearances can damage a brand's appeal.

The reason behind this is classic Pavlovian psychology. When new or unexpected stimuli reach the brain, the *orienting reflex* reacts in response. If the same stimulus is repeated, the orienting reflex habituates or gets used to the stimulus, and the novelty is lost.

Pop star Ricky Martin burst onto the music scene in 1999 and seemed to be everywhere at once—even on the inaugural stage with George W. Bush. He quickly saturated the media, and the general public began to tire of seeing him. By overexposing himself in the beginning, and with no new pop hit to regenerate his popularity, Martin's star has diminished.

Visibility Through Leveraging Opportunity

This option says, "Be ready when opportunity knocks." It refers to a Personal Brand source being prepared to take advantage when opportunities for visibility appear.

Vermont Senator James Jeffords threw the Republican-controlled Senate into chaos in 2001 when he abruptly announced his intention to become an Independent, thereby giving Democrats a fifty to

---

*Want to gain visibility? E-mail your best visibility tactic to personalbranding@petermontoya.com and it may appear in my monthly publication, *Personal Branding*.

forty-nine advantage and control of the upper house of Congress. Clearly, Jeffords had examined the possible consequences of his switch and planned his move carefully, waiting for the right time. When he shook the powers that be with his announcement, visibility was not his motivation; he stated it was a matter of conscience. However, visibility he got, along with a vastly higher profile as a Washington mover and shaker.

Leveraging opportunity involves two steps:

- Researching the possible future chances for visibility and publicity in the domain.

- Preparing the resources to make the most of those chances when they arise.

Pitfall: Missed Opportunities

Being *reactive* when it comes to visibility means wasted resources and missed opportunities. Sometimes the cause is laziness; in other instances, it's the result of not understanding the value of visibility in developing a Personal Brand. Either way, if you don't grab the opportunity, your competition will.

As told by author Tom Wolfe in *The Right Stuff*, the story of Pete Conrad, who *almost* became one of the original seven astronauts, is a classic example of missed opportunity, despite great qualification. Ace fighter jock Conrad was a prime candidate, but his wicked sense of humor and constant gags did not impress the humorless doctors or military men conducting the tests to determine who the seven would be. In the end, Conrad was rejected as "not suitable for long-duration space flight"—not serious enough. He was later chosen for the second group of astronauts, but when it came to being on the same pinnacle as Alan Shepard and John Glenn, he missed out.

Visibility by Accident

Accidental visibility occurs when a person is interviewed for an article, wins an unexpected award, has a chance encounter with a person of influence and so on. It is potentially scary because accidental visibility implies that you cannot control how you will be perceived. That is not entirely true, but the likelihood of drawing attention that is beyond your control highlights the importance of the other Laws.

The only way to prepare for and draw value from accidental visibility is to build a "bulletproof" Personal Brand: authentic, reflective of the real person underneath, consistent and designed to appeal to its domain. In effect, living the Personal Brand is the best defense against surprise.

Colleen Haskell, one of the original castaways in everybody's favorite bit of voyeurism named for a cheeseball '80s rock band, *Survivor*, turned her thirty days of television visibility into a blockbuster film role. Likable and sporting a girl-next-door appeal, she landed the romantic female lead role in the 2001 Rob Schneider comedy *The Animal*, a break she admits she didn't plan on. Despite having no acting experience, she had seemed so sweet and genuine that even the notorious Hollywood machine treated her with kindness.

Pitfall: Avoidance

Nothing raises suspicion like someone who pleads the Fifth Amendment, the one that prohibits self-implication in a court of law. People who avoid questions are assumed to have something to hide, and that's what happens to people who duck accidental visibility because they are afraid of the impression they'll make.

Preparation is the best guard against this. Second best is simply being flexible and trying to make the best impression. Even with this, the odds are better; the old college try is bound to impress a part of the target audience, while avoidance impresses no one.

J.D. Salinger, author of *The Catcher in the Rye*, withdrew from public life after the success of his early works, leaving a hungry public without an interview or a clue as to his future writing plans, if any. Salinger's curmudgeonly exile has made him something of a cult figure, but he has surely missed out on fame and fortune. Not that he seems to care.

There Is Such a Thing as Bad Publicity

Ask Monica Lewinsky. Ask O.J. Simpson. Those who claim bad publicity doesn't exist are engaging in a dangerous game of denial. Negative publicity damages a Personal Brand in many ways, none more insidious than rumor and gossip. Claims of fact can be fought with logic, but there's no defense for rumor ingrained in a domain's culture.

For example, during the 2000 presidential campaign, rumors began circulating about George W. Bush's supposed drug problems. True or not (they were bolstered by his admission of past transgressions), the rumors that followed him during the election continue to harm his image to this day.

Is negative publicity worse than no publicity? Yes, because it stains the blank slate all Personal Brands start with. With no publicity, you are free to shape perception as you will. Negative publicity forces you to *erase* before you can begin shaping. And sometimes, erasing is impossible.

Fighting Bad Publicity

Here, an ounce of prevention is definitely worth a pound of cure. However, if the publicity black horse has already fled the barn, there are things you can do:

- **Identify the source:** Find the source of the negative information— a company, a person, an organization.

- **Get the story:** Find out exactly what is being said: who, what, where, when and so on. Be an investigative reporter.

- **Assess the damage:** How deeply into your domain has the information penetrated? To surface contacts or centers of influence?

- **Strategize:** Develop a plan for dealing with the publicity, rather than simply reacting.

- **Own up:** If the story is true, confess. The truth always comes out, so you can minimize damage by telling it first.

- **Counterattack:** If the story is false, counter with information. That may be issuing a press release, e-mailing key contacts to refute a story, or filing a lawsuit. A strong denial works wonders.

- **Produce positively:** Whether a story is true or false, the best way to put it behind you is to keep working and producing quality.

Public Scrutiny Is Inevitable

Regrettably, we're a talk show society. We adore dirt. Most people love a sordid story far more than an uplifting one. And when you place a Personal Brand in the public eye, you're also placing it in the public crosshairs. Scrutiny is inevitable—if there is something to come out, it will come out.

Are you ready for life under a microscope? Find out by answering a few questions:

- Are there any buried secrets you think are safe from prying eyes?

- Are there enemies or people who would spread malicious rumors?

- Could it look to outsiders like you are hiding something, even if that is not the case?

Obeying the Law of Visibility

- **Form a visibility strategy:** Get out and research the opportunities in your domain to be seen and heard—speaking engagements, mailing lists, awards entries, trade journals and so on. Assess your Personal Brand goals, match them to the appropriate opportunities, and get the facts on how to get visible through those means.

- **Take credit without burning bridges:** One of the fastest ways to be seen and noticed is to get credit for a positive accomplishment, but such credit can also alienate others. The key? Actively seek and accept recognition while *simultaneously* giving credit to others who played a role. This positions you as both achiever and leader.

- **Manage accessibility:** Celebrities have publicists who manage their availability. Why? The harder a person is to get, the more desirable he is perceived as being. In a profession, taking every project and being available for every meeting can create the impression that you are not discriminating about the work you take on. Appearing choosy and not always being available (even if you are) makes you more desirable and gives you greater control of your time.

- **Consistency vs. reinvention:** Consistency is one of the foundation stones of a great Personal Brand. But you can reinvent tiny portions of your brand from time to time to keep it fresh. It's like putting new wheel covers on a BMW: the car is the same, but there's a new bit of flash that makes people take notice. While keeping the essence of a Personal Brand consistent, try adding new skills, a new look or even a new marketing message once in a while.

Madonna
Queen of Self-Reinvention

There is no smarter, more daring, more relentless master of self-promotion than Madonna Louise Ciccone, the Catholic girl from the Detroit suburbs. Say what you will about her musical talent, she has made herself an object of fascination, desire and controversy the world over, by the force of her business savvy and her marketing brilliance. Madonna is Personal Branding personified.

Madonna [1958 –]

Born in 1958 near Detroit, Madonna Ciccone was the eldest daughter of an engineer father and a housewife mother who died of cancer when Madonna was six. The outoing girl's passion for showbiz led her to sign up for school shows, cheerleading, piano lessons and ballet classes.

Madonna's dancing skills earned her a scholarship to the University of Michigan. In 1978, two years into her studies, she grew impatient for stardom, dropped out and moved to New York. According to the popular story, she landed in Times Square with thirty-five dollars and her ambition.

After some low-wage jobs, Madonna landed some short-lived gigs with the acclaimed Alvin Ailey and Martha Graham dance ensembles. But before long, her interests turned to music. The dancer-singer joined a succession of bands, and during the early 1980s tried her hand at writing songs. DJ Mark Kamins gave Madonna her big break: he created a club-scene hit from one of her demo singles, "Everybody," and introduced the budding starlet to Warner Bros. executives, who promptly signed her to a recording contract.

How This Brand Was Built

Madonna's entire rise is a lesson in self-promotion, designed to maximize her visibility and the public's bewitchment with her—a twenty-year series of carefully calculated moves designed to titillate, stun and provoke. As a provocateur, she has done everything she can to put her name on people's lips, from publishing her controversial book *Sex,* building masturbation into the choreography for her 1990 Blond Ambition Tour, to trying to insure her breasts for $6 million each.

Madonna's secrets? Her absolute lack of apology for her outrageous acts and her chameleon-like talent for reinventing herself. She has been sex siren, material girl, defender of the First Amendment, movie star, earth mother, and so many other identities it's a wonder she can keep them straight. Her constant metamorphoses keep her fresh even into the twenty-first century. Despite her many faces, she has remained true to her leading attribute: the female trendsetter for the media world.

Why This Brand Works

- **Audacity:** Madonna is always bold and daring, even when doing something she knows will earn the disapproval of much of the public. When she does something, she does it big.

- **Originality:** Some pop stars do movies. Madonna did *Evita.* Some write autobiographies. She published *Sex,* a dirty picture book. Whatever Madonna does to gain visibility and recharge her flagging popularity, it's always unique.

- **Consistency:** Consistent? But she changes her identity every year! True, and that is her consistency. Madonna is known as a master of disguise, and it's expected of her. Her consistency at reinventing herself is her most powerful Personal Brand attribute.

- **Sensuality:** We're not just talking about sex here, but the primal appeal Madonna has for men and women. Some men lust after her, some respect her guts and some want her wardrobe. Women can't look away even as they are repelled by her, fascinated by her power to control instead of being controlled.

Adherence to the Eight Laws

1. **The Law of Specialization.** Madonna still practices her craft. She spends hours writing, recording and being the best performer possible.

2. **The Law of Leadership.** When she launched her 2001 tour she was adamant that it was not going to be a "Greatest Hits" tour. Twenty years after hitting the scene, she is still on the cutting edge.

3. **The Law of Personality.** Her true personality is muddled after all these years, but what you see is what you get. She is very authentic and her personality is evident in every aspect of her career.

4. **The Law of Distinctiveness.** No one else in the 1980s approached the world of pop music with the unabashed sexuality of Madonna, and she has only grown that provocative identity in the years since. She is synonymous with self-reinvention and promotion.

5. **The Law of Visibility.** If there was a higher ranking, she would get it. Madonna's ability to keep herself in the news and in the public consciousness makes up for her breaking of other laws.

6. **The Law of Unity.** With so many changes and so much promotion, who knows who the woman behind closed doors is? Every indication is what you see is what you get.

7. **The Law of Persistence.** She has never wavered from her mission to keep pushing the envelope of what is tasteful, sexy and tolerable—all the face of censorship, denouncement and disdain.

8. **The Law of Goodwill.** Ask people what they think of Madonna, and you will hear a lot of, "I don't like her music, but I respect what she's done as a self-promoter." That is common. Many people like her as a woman who has, through her own will and skill, carved her name on a man's world in big letters.

Influence in Its Domain

Few pop stars have a lasting influence on culture or society, but within her domain of entertainment, Madonna has created waves. Her X-rated exploits have helped usher in a new era of sexual frankness—and some would say, taken us farther down the slippery slope to exploitation and trash culture. Either way, she has changed things.

CHAPTER NINE

Law Six: The Law of Unity

The source of a great Personal Brand must exhibit private behavior that matches the brand's public persona.

In the Law of Personality, we discussed *authenticity*—building a Personal Brand that reflects the character, abilities and values of its source. Unity is its kissing cousin, surpassing it in one crucial aspect: if broken, this law has more potential than any other to destroy a brand.

The Law of Unity states that the private person behind a Personal Brand must adhere to the moral and behavioral code set down by that brand. Private conduct must mirror public brand; it won't do to pitch family values to a domain while throwing wild sex parties behind closed doors. Flouting this law risks disaster as your audience pays you back for not being who you appear to be.

Fooling Some of the People...

Is it possible to fool some of the people some of the time? Of course—look at Congress: men and women showing one face to their constituents while wearing another in closed meetings where power is brokered. But the fact remains you cannot build a great, lasting Personal Brand without unity. The truth always comes out.

Example: Jesse Jackson, a self-proclaimed pillar of values and defender of the downtrodden, shook his believers in 2000 when he confessed to having fathered a child out of wedlock. For this volubly Christian man, engaging in such un-Christian behavior has damaged his reputation far more than accusations of headline chasing.

Is unity really necessary in an age of synthesized pop music stars? Yes, because no image, no matter how precisely crafted and jealously protected, is flawless. Public life is unpredictable, and there is no way to know what surprises will test a Personal Brand. Stories get out, gossip circulates, reporters report.

If a public brand is built around values or behavior that run counter to the way the source acts in private, eventually there will be a catastrophic slip. It is inevitable. Unity ensures that a Personal Brand can endure long-term public exposure.

Assumed and Natural Behavior

There are two types of behaviors associated with a Personal Brand:

- Assumed Behaviors—taken on to make the brand more attractive to its domain

- Natural Behaviors—already part of the source's behavioral set

In a perfect world, every Personal Brand would be based on natural behaviors. But sometimes appealing to an audience means adopting a new characteristic: learning a second language or trying a new style of dress.

That is acceptable, as long as the assumed behavior doesn't stray too far from core values or behaviors. When there is a disconnect, when a white suburban Boy Scout dresses like an inner-city thug and carries a gun to fit into "gangsta rap" culture, there is trouble on the horizon.

Rock Hudson hid his homosexuality during his entire film career, knowing such a revelation in less-tolerant times would ruin him. His career was over by the time the story broke, but it still cast a pall of bad jokes and hate mail during the last years of his life.

The Three Zones

There's a saying, "Character is what you do when no one is watching." The key to creating unity is to build a brand the source can live when no one is watching.

A Personal Brand is lived in three "zones":

1. **Relationships**

2. **Finances**

3. **Conduct**

- **Relationships:** Significant others, friends, family, colleagues and clients are all part of this zone. Unity here is largely a matter of creating public expectations the source can live with in private. A person known for treating subordinates with kindness cannot become Genghis Khan at home or on vacation.

- **Finances:** This zone involves spending habits, debt, generosity (or lack of it) and honesty. Money breeds scandal in direct proportion to the amount, so it is crucial to avoid the appearance of impropriety. A big spender in public cannot have his kids wearing hand-me-downs, while fudging on private finances creates suspicion that the same is going on in business.

- **Conduct:** Public actions, personality, clothing, possessions and speech all fit into this zone. This is a matter of managing perceptions. Wear $100,000 in gold jewelry and your domain may assume you are priced out of their range, when at home you are a jeans and t-shirts man. Or they may embrace you. It depends on the domain.

Live Your Personal Brand

There are two ways to create a disunited Personal Brand: assume behaviors that you know will contradict your private life, or assume behaviors you think you can maintain privately, but cannot. Whether you are lying to others or yourself, the effect is the same: a Personal Brand you cannot live with.

It is a dangerous state to be in, because every audience has a "Phony Meter," used to gauge the truth of any person's words, actions and identity. The more you spike the needle on the meter, the wider the perception that you are not what you appear to be. Bury the needle and you'll suffer serious consequences:

• Audience anger at the realization they have been lied to

• Attempts at retribution—taking away business, professional sanctions, legal action

• Destruction of all credibility within your domain

We know the details of the "trial of the century." But, the fact remains, O.J. Simpson was found not guilty. So why is he reviled by society? Aside from the belief that he did commit the grisly murders, public disgust with Simpson stems from courtroom revelations that the beloved former football star, commentator and *Naked Gun* actor was anything but a hero in real life: allegedly abusive, possessive and mentally unstable. When illusions shatter, jagged shards cut deep.

If a Personal Brand and its source have a track record within a domain, they can survive minor inconsistencies. Major disconnects—criminal acts, lewd behavior, taking credit for another's work—will usually sink any Personal Brand, no matter how well-known and trusted.

Pitfall: Hypocrisy

No one epitomizes the perils of being a smiling liar more than former President Bill Clinton. Perhaps the most charming man to
occupy the White House in the twentieth century, he nonetheless
bore a film of moral corrosion and infidelity even before he entered
office in 1993. Many of us suspected, but his ebullient personality
and bold initiatives fooled a lot of people.

The suspicions appeared with Gennifer Flowers, grew with Paula
Jones and blew up in America's face with Monica Lewinsky. When
Clinton went before the independent prosecutor to respond to
charges that he had engaged in sexual relations with Lewinsky and
then covered it up, he did the worst thing possible: he morphed into
Slick Willie. He prevaricated, he argued about the meaning of "is"
and of a sex act. He made a fool of himself, and in the process he
destroyed much of the trust and respect of the American people.

True, Clinton survived impeachment and finished his term.
But if the true measure of a president is his legacy and what the
historians say, Clinton's legacy will forever be that of the smug,
smiling liar.

Obeying the Law of Unity

• **Prepare to give up some freedom:** This is one of the prices often
paid when a person becomes a Personal Brand. Depending on the
values and tastes of a domain, success might mean trading a behavior that just doesn't fit the audience: wild partying, a dangerous
hobby or a fiery temper might have to be boxed up and put in stor-
age. That is why it's so vital to learn what a domain will and will
not tolerate, and ask yourself "What am I willing to give up?" Never
give up what you will regret later; a Personal Brand should not be
a life sentence.

- **Start natural and adjust:** In the beginning, learn what will appeal to and offend the domain in question, and assess whether or not natural behaviors will work. Don't assume any behaviors for the sake of a domain if it is not necessary; it makes the Personal Brand more livable and united. If some aspects of natural behavior don't get it done, such as casual dress or vulgar speech, start adjusting gradually and systematically. Slowly formalizing attire, or taking a speech class, and working the changes in gradually, will not shock the audience, and will make the changes easier to maintain.

- **Check long-term livability:** A Personal Brand must be livable day-to-day with minimal effort. Keep an eye out for warning signs of non-livability:

  - Private behavior that is at the opposite extreme from the brand

  - Feelings of pressure to keep up the facade

  - Constant "tweaking" of assumed behavior—
    it's never quite right

  - Feeling of being imprisoned by the Personal Brand

If you see any of these signs, the Personal Brand is disunited. Take a close look at what is being done to appeal to the domain and how you can change it to be more in line with the source's tastes, values and personality.

Personal Brand Profile

Albert Einstein

The Genius

The face. That wild-haired face with its grandfatherly landscape of wrinkles. Those deep eyes that appeared as if they could peer behind the curtain of reality...which, in effect, they did. Few faces from the twentieth century are as memorable as that of Albert Einstein. Theoretical physicist, progenitor of the atomic bomb, ladies' man and kindly Princeton professor, cult figure—these all describe the man whose extraordinary mind changed how we perceive the universe, and whose name has come to be synonymous with genius.

Albert Einstein (1879-1955)

Born in Ulm, Germany on March 14, 1879, Einstein spent his youth in Munich, where his family owned a small shop that manufactured electric machinery. When repeated business failure led the family to leave Germany for Milan, Italy, Einstein, who was then fifteen, withdrew from the schools of Munich. He stayed a year with his parents in Milan, then left to finish secondary school in Arrau, Switzerland, and entered the Swiss National Polytechnic in Zürich.

Again the schools didn't satisfy Einstein's independent intellect. He often cut classes and used the time to study physics on his own or to play violin. He graduated in 1900 but his professors disliked him and wouldn't recommend him for a position in the university. In 1902 he secured a position as an examiner in a Swiss patent office in Bern.

In 1905, Einstein received his doctorate from the University of Zürich for a theoretical dissertation on the dimensions of molecules. This same year, he also published three theoretical papers which would catapult him to the forefront of twentieth-century physics.

How This Brand Was Built

Einstein built his brand in the most unforgiving arena of all: the world of early twentieth-century science, where every new theory had to withstand the most rigorous, skeptical examination. But even in that environment, his 1905 Special Theory of Relativity, which argued that space and time are not absolutes but vary with circumstances, and his 1915 General Theory of Relativity, which presented $E = MC^2$, were hailed as transcendent genius, if controversial and yet to be proved.

Einstein's prestige took a quantum leap when, over the next twenty years, his relativity experiments were proved to be correct. A German Jew, he also became a renowned pacifist, and emigrated to America in 1933 after Adolf Hitler became Chancellor of Germany. As a professor at Princeton, Einstein gained greater visibility, becoming widely known as a violin-playing raconteur. Privately, he continued to seek a unified theory for all forces in the universe, and contradicted his own pacifist views by urging President Franklin D. Roosevelt to step up research on the atomic bomb. A complex, brilliant man, he remained the symbol of genius to a generation of Americans until his death in 1955.

Why This Brand Works

- **Vision:** Einstein gained the glamour that no other scientist of his time could match simply because with relativity, he redefined reality. Instead of talking about neutrinos or rotating quasars, Einstein talked about time, something we can all identify with. His ideas had tremendous appeal, though no more than a handful of people on earth understood their full implications.

- **Appeal:** Einstein was the original crazy-haired absentminded professor, a beloved archetype. He played the violin, he rode a bicycle, he appeared in a famous photo with his tongue stuck out like an eight-year-old—all these things endeared him to the public.

- **Mystery:** He had an astonishing intellect, so much so that he taught himself calculus and the higher sciences at age sixteen. Since his death, generations have been fascinated with an intellect capable of dissecting workings of a reality no one else could even perceive—so fascinated that until recently, the pathologist who removed Einstein's brain after his death kept the brain in Tupperware at his home, sending slices off to researchers around the globe for analysis.

- **Appearance:** Einstein looked like no one else: the shock of white hair, the mustache and beard, the soulful eyes. His unique visage continues to adorn posters, shirts and books to this day.

Adherence to the Eight Laws

1. **The Law of Specialization.** Einstein was just one of many young physicists in Europe...until he published his revolutionary works about relativity. Then he became a genius to some, a father of controversy to others, but known to all.

2. **The Law of Leadership.** He stood at the pinnacle of the scientific community after his theories were proven right—and remains so today, as current scientists test and re-test relativity only to find that its principles stand up.

3. **The Law of Personality.** Einstein had no real ambition to be a public figure, so he did not conceal his real self. He was a somewhat

sad, lonely man in private life, though most outside his close circle only knew him as "the genius."

4. **The Law of Distinctiveness.** From his looks to his Princeton social life, to his winning the Nobel Prize in 1921, Einstein stood out among scientists as a humanist, a fun-loving gent and a true original.

5. **The Law of Visibility.** The fame his work on relativity produced, coupled with his vocal advocacy for disarmament, kept him in the public eye throughout most of his life.

6. **The Law of Unity.** The real Einstein was behind closed doors, working long into the night on equations 99.99 percent of the earth's population could not even comprehend. This serious, highly driven man was at odds with the sweet, witty rogue that he became in his public life. Both were the real Einstein, but both were quite separate.

7. **The Law of Persistence.** Einstein never tried to manipulate his image. He didn't care; he had his causes—disarmament and the discovery of a unified field theory. His mission and his devotion to it never wavered, so much so that on his deathbed he was scribbling equations.

8. **The Law of Goodwill.** A few anti-Semites blamed Einstein for the A-bomb because of his $E = MC^2$ equation. Most of the world simply regarded him as a treasure: a great, gentle genius.

Influence in Its Domain

Einstein's ruminations on time, space, the speed of light and gravity changed the universe and our place in it. His theories, which have now held up for more than eight decades, continue to be one of two principles underpinning all modern physics. It is safe to say his influence was incalculable.

CHAPTER TEN

Law Seven: The Law of Persistence

Great Personal Brands require time, consistency of direction and a determined rejection of fads and trends.

Money can't buy a Personal Brand. It doesn't matter if you spend it on billboards and full-page ads, you'll be wasting it. Those promotional tactics can help, of course, but they're no substitute for the only force with the power to build your brand: Time.

The Law of Persistence states that any Personal Brand takes time to grow, and while you can accelerate the process, you can't replace it with advertising or public relations. You've got to stick with it, be unwavering and be patient.

Think of the greatest Personal Brands: Tiger Woods, Oprah Winfrey and so on. They have taken years to become icons, and they are supported by many years of sacrifice, achievement and planning.* Great Personal Brands seem to spring out of nowhere, but they're really springing into wide public awareness after a long period of dedicated work and brand building. It's like the twenty-year veteran actor who became an "overnight success."

There are no shortcuts to creating a powerful Personal Brand, just as there are none in building a muscular body. In fact, the two are very similar: they both demand steady work, dedication and the patience to persist even though results are slow in coming. Neither

---

*Are you a twenty-year "overnight" success? What did you sacrifice? What challenge did you overcome? Share your story with me by e-mailing personalbranding@petermontoya.com and it may appear in my publication, *Personal Branding*.

is glamorous, and the results are so gradual that it may be hard to see progress.

However, just as you'll look in the mirror one day and see rock-hard biceps and pecs, you'll go to the office one day to discover business has boomed for you. When a Personal Brand hits after long years of development, the results can be dramatic.

First-Mover Advantage

I'm not saying a well-designed brand won't benefit you almost immediately; it probably will. But a Personal Brand that dominates its domain and helps you achieve your goals or gains nationwide exposure takes time.

This is all the more the reason to start building early, staking out brand territory with a specialized identity before anyone else in the target domain does. We have already discussed first-mover advantage—being first is the way to get it. Some skeptics say the first-mover is usually the one to make all the mistakes, and those who follow learn from those errors. I disagree. Being first does create vulnerabilities, but also allows you to capture *mind share* immediately and be perceived as the first in a category. That is powerful.

Consistency over Time Builds Trust

The other big advantage to launching a Personal Brand sooner rather than later is simple: your brand has more time to develop. Building a great Personal Brand takes time because humans distrust people who appear manufactured; we hold more positive feelings about Personal Brands that develop *organically*—subject to the natural effects of time, trial and chance. As with wine, we trust people who have aged, blended their flaws into strengths and acquired unexpected notes that have nothing to do with market research.

Persistent Personal Brands

Here's the good news: Evidence suggests that Personal Brands that build longer before hitting it big also stay at their peak longer. Some examples:

- **John Lee Hooker:** The late blues legend played the rough dives and swank clubs for decades, and in his eighties had become hipper and cooler than ever.

- **John Wooden:** The iconic former UCLA basketball coach had so much success people started to take it for granted, but now, as an elder statesman and speaker, his wisdom is treasured.

- **Jimmy Carter:** While in office he was derided as a fuzzy-minded Georgia peanut farmer. Since leaving, he has become lauded as a great humanitarian and force for peace.

- **Ted Turner:** Brash and unwilling to listen, he was an egotistical self-promoter with insane ideas. Then he founded CNN and the Goodwill Games. Now he's an oracle.

- **Toni Morrison:** She has been publishing poetry, novels, essays and literary criticism since 1970, but it wasn't until 1993, when she received the Nobel Prize for Literature, that she began to assume the mantle of national treasure that she wears today.

Slow to Create—Never Deviate

That is the Personal Branding mantra. Even if you follow all the other laws to perfection, the brand you create will still take time to develop. Never stop promoting it, and never change it on a whim because of impatience. Stick with the brand identity and traits you have established and ignore trends, criticism and self-doubt. Only then will the brand have time to penetrate the audience's consciousness.

Pitfall: Sudden Change

The temptation is understandable: the brand is slow to develop, results are small, impatience is rising. But suddenly changing a Personal Brand's course after months or years of projecting an identity does nothing but confuse an audience. As we have established, you can't change a mind that's already made up. In making radical, midstream revisions to a brand, you send an entire new set of perceptions crashing against previously set perceptions. The result is wreckage.

Boxer Oscar de la Hoya's career as the "Golden Boy" began with great promise: rising out of the *barrios* of East Los Angeles, winning an Olympic gold medal and capturing world titles in several weight classes. Then he decided he would retire and become an architect...then he donned leather pants and recorded a pop CD...then he decided to go back to his roots, all the while derided by his working-class Latino neighbors as a pretty boy sellout. What is Oscar de la Hoya? No one is really sure.

Make It a Lifelong Passion

In creating your own Personal Brand, begin with something that stirs your passions. A lifelong passion makes it immensely easier to give a Personal Brand the time it needs to grow. *Cherished brands are built by people working for long years at a labor of love, promoting themselves minimally, letting the quality of their work do the talking, refining and becoming the best at what they do.* Only passion makes that possible.

Adversity tempers the strongest people, and their Personal Brands with them. Would Nelson Mandela have become an icon for the struggle against oppression without spending twenty-seven years in prison? Overcoming adversity has given his brand greatness and power few can match. You don't need to go to prison for your Personal Brand; merely understand that tribulations are part of its development.

Self-Confidence

This is where most Personal Brand plans hit the wall. The source is fine until something shakes his confidence: a slowdown in business, criticism of his image or the pressure of cultural change. And he caves—doubting, changing or killing his brand.

Opposition and naysayers are a part of Personal Brand development. Not everyone will understand or like the brand you create; take that as a sign that it is being noticed. Sound planning, domain research, goal setting, understanding your audience and, above all, building a Personal Brand based on authentic strengths—these all provide the confidence needed to outlast the opposition.

Pitfall: Quitting

Nobody likes a quitter. That's third grade wisdom. Abandoning the development of a healthy brand sets you back to square one and can make you appear flaky. It is much wiser to adjust midstream. As much as consistency and the ability to persevere are admired, the habit of jumping ship as soon as seas get choppy is reviled.

Ross Perot reveals the perils of quitting: In 1992, the brash Texas businessman entered the presidential race as an independent, claiming he could address the needs of the American people. But, on the way to building his new Personal Brand—the odd, plain-speaking country boy who bucked the system—Perot abruptly dropped out of the race in July, only to re-enter three weeks before the election. This flip-flopping became his legacy in the minds of many Americans, and he hasn't been taken seriously in politics since.

The Personal Brand Evolution

Every Personal Brand follows a predictable path from inception to the point where it "hits"—penetrates its domain and creates awareness and affinity. Each step is fraught with its own challenges and opportunities, but knowing the steps provides a clearer understanding of how a Personal Brand evolves.

1. **Brand creation:** The source or marketer decides on the brand identity, the domain, core traits and values that will be promoted.

2. **Crafting the "leading attribute" message:** The brand's creator develops the words, images or key behaviors that will communicate the brand's leading attribute (creativity, dependability, inventiveness, etc.).

3. **Message number one:** The initial message from the new Personal Brand hits the domain…and barely makes a ripple.

4. **Adjusting Message number one:** The creator fine-tunes the message to compensate for misjudgments or negative feedback.

5. **Message number one filters into domain culture:** The target audience has absorbed the adjusted Message number one; its small effect has been felt.

6. **Message number two:** The creator produces and sends a new, complementary message into the domain, where it has a greater effect than the first.

7. **Message number one dies:** It goes stale, runs out of steam and vanishes.

8. **Adjusting Message number two:** The creator fine-tunes the second message based on experience with Message number one and new feedback from the domain.

9. **Message number two filters into domain culture:** The target audience has absorbed the message and become more familiar with the Personal Brand; effects are more pronounced.

10. **Message number three:** The creator produces a third, more precise and sophisticated message based on the knowledge gained from Messages number one and number two. This message has a still greater effect.

11. **Message number two dies:** It gets too familiar, loses novelty and fades out.

12. **Message number three takes hold:** This message has gained momentum from the first two and penetrated the cognitive clutter of the domain.

13. **Brand awareness begins:** With strong, consistent messaging, the audience knows the Personal Brand, perceives the values it stands for and has developed an emotional response to it. Awareness is in place and the Personal Brand should thrive.

    Of course, this evolution only applies when the Personal Brand is supported with goal setting, domain research and persistent, effective messaging. Notice that one message is never enough; it takes multiple exposures to get past the domain's surface.

Obeying the Law of Persistence

- **Take time to craft the brand:** If you believe in something, you will invest more time to ensure that it works. Spend as much time crafting the Personal Brand as the process demands. Putting in the time on research, refinement of attributes and promotional strategies will result in a brand you can spend time building without losing interest.

- **Manage your expectations:** Before dropping your first message on the target domain, decide how long you will allow for results. Setting realistic timelines for the steps of the Personal Brand's development helps keep you focused. And if you see results earlier, consider it a bonus.

- **Keep promoting even if there are no results:** This is the most important advice. Results may not be evident in the first few months after you launch the brand, which is normal. There is a great deal of "noise" in any domain, and it takes time for people to perceive a Personal Brand, no matter how compelling. Push on even when the phone isn't ringing. It will.

- **Schedule fine-tuning:** Following the Personal Brand Evolution, schedule dates to analyze and refine your Personal Brand. By talking to people in the target domain and evaluating your experiences, you will be able to identify areas in which the brand is missing its mark—appearing too similar to a competitor, not making an emotional connection and so on. This allows you to make fine—not major—adjustments in attributes and messages.

Personal Brand Profile

Larry King
King of the Talk Show

CNN's gravelly-voiced call-in show host has been interviewing people for more than forty years, but he only became an "overnight" success in 1985 after the debut of *Larry King Live*. Journalists come and go, but King has built a unique Personal Brand—the worldly-wise, hard-nosed reporter with a heart of gold—through years of honing his skills during over 40,000 interviews. He has made time his greatest ally.

Larry King [1933 –   ]

Born in Brooklyn in 1933 as Larry Zeiger, King lost his father, a bar owner, at age nine, and his mother had to go on welfare to support Larry and his younger brother. Discouraged by his father's death, King let his schoolwork lapse, throwing cold water on any aspirations for college. Instead, after graduating from high school, he went to work to help support his mother. But from an early age, he had dreamed of a career in radio, and haunted the radio studios of New York.

After a chance meeting with a CBS staff announcer, King took the older man's advice and caught a bus for Florida, where a rapidly growing media market was creating an opening for newer, less experienced radio personalities. After some initial setbacks, King got his first break as a disc jockey on a Miami station and soon became a popular fixture on the South Florida radio scene.

How This Brand Was Built

King's Personal Brand rests on a bed of experience. As far back as the 1970s he was a popular radio talk show host in Miami, but his irascible temper, his blunt but polite style of questioning and his clear skill as an interviewer earned him a national audience in 1978. With the muscle of CNN behind him, he has gained access to some of the most important personalities on the world stage, from presidents (he has interviewed all the living ones) to world leaders like Yasser Arafat to notably reclusive celebrities like Barbara Streisand.

The other side of King's brand coin is his perseverance through well-publicized heart problems. At age sixty-nine, he continues to exhibit vigor despite multiple heart attacks and heart surgeries, not only continuing to work a full schedule but contributing time and effort to such pet causes as public affairs reporting, the March of Dimes and the Larry King Cardiac Foundation.

Why This Brand Works

- **Excellence:** Strip away everything else and it's unanimous: Larry King is a hell of an interviewer. He is one of the most respected broadcast journalists in the world, a status he has earned with polished skills, a fine-tuned investigative sensibility and well-honed instinct. Plus, he has won enough journalism awards to sink the QE2. No wonder he gets guests who will not appear anywhere else.

- **Visibility:** He is on the world's largest news network five nights a week talking with the famous and infamous about world affairs and personal scandals. It's the rare adult who doesn't see King at least on occasion, which is why he has become a sort of byword for courting the mass media: "Well, next thing she'll be on *Larry King Live*."

- **Authenticity:** King is the antithesis of the blow-dried manikins who serve up most of the television news on the local level. He's past retirement age, his face is lined, he hunches over the microphone, he's raspy and abrupt, and he's mortal, as multiple heart problems have shown. In short, he is one of us.

- **Altruism:** King's public service is well-known, and it makes him appear even more to be a man interested in public welfare. From programming on depression for the American Foundation for Suicide Prevention to the Save the Children Foundation, he has embraced numerous worthwhile causes and used his powerful pulpit to spread the word to the nation. We have embraced him for it.

Adherence to the Eight Laws

1. **The Law of Specialization.** King is a leader in a field that is sparsely populated: the true journalist interviewer. He continues to sharpen his skills to this day.

2. **The Law of Leadership.** He has received virtually every honor for excellence the journalism and television communities can award, and has been called "the Muhammad Ali" of the broadcast interview. He is the unquestioned best in his business.

3. **The Law of Personality.** King's gravelly voice, his pointed shoulders, his bluntness, his tendency to talk over callers he thinks are asking dumb questions and all of his small flaws are part of his grander whole.

4. **The Law of Distinctiveness.** Nobody has the on-air persona of King, and no interviewer matches his aura of rapt attention while being poised to pounce on a contradiction or a juicy line of thinking. He is unique.

5. **The Law of Visibility.** King is in front of millions of viewers five nights a week. The biggest names in politics, show business and the media sit across the table from him. He is among the most visible people in the world.

6. **The Law of Unity.** His battles with heart disease have been no mystery, nor have his multiple marriages. King knows that his journalistic credentials can stand on their own no matter what happens in his personal life, so he makes no effort to conceal it.

7. **The Law of Persistence.** Forty years in the profession show that King has paid his dues and developed his extraordinary interviewing skills through trial and error. He has earned his place at the top of the pyramid.

8. **The Law of Goodwill.** His efforts on behalf of numerous charities and worthwhile organizations only add to our culture's positive feelings towards him.

Influence in Its Domain

Larry King has built a platform on which the powerful, the beautiful and the ridiculous can speak their minds to the American people. For better or worse, when there is a message to send or a story to tell, *Larry King Live* is the first place the newsmakers go.

CHAPTER ELEVEN

Law Eight: The Law of Goodwill

A great Personal Brand must be perceived as well-intentioned or embodying positive values if it is to maximize its influence.

Finally, we get down to being liked. Herein lies the difference between a great Personal Brand and a powerful one—whether or not your domain sees you as a good person. Compared with authenticity, consistency and the other laws, this may seem lightweight. But it is serious; people do business with people they like.

The Law of Goodwill states that a Personal Brand will produce better results and endure longer if the person behind it is perceived in a positive way. That does not mean every source needs to be feeding orphans or protecting baby seals, but it does mean he or she must be associated with a value or idea that is recognized universally as positive and worthwhile.

Why Goodwill Matters

Shouldn't what you can do, not how warm and fuzzy you are, have the greatest bearing on the success of your Personal Brand? In a logical world, yes. But domains are made of human beings, and we are not logical. We want to work with the most skilled engineer, the savviest political consultant or the best movie director. But, we also want to work with people whom we respect, whose company we enjoy and who make us look good to others. So when it comes to a decision between two comparable individuals, the best person—not the best talent—often wins.

This isn't always the case; plenty of tyrannical film directors have fifty-year careers. But it's pervasive enough to make goodwill a force. Cultivating goodwill—respect, admiration, love, identification or even compassion—can tip the scales in an otherwise even contest.

Exhibiting Goodwill

You don't need to shelter the homeless to gain goodwill. In fact, over-doing kindness can backfire and leave you looking self-serving. There are better ways to earn that positive aura:

- **Embody a positive value:** Hard work, the will to win and self-improvement are all values Americans cherish, and by bringing one of them out in a Personal Brand, you associate it with the source. But the value must be part of the source to begin with. Magic Johnson worked tirelessly for years to improve as an NBA player, led the Los Angeles Lakers to multiple championships, then showed endearing courage when he publicly announced his HIV infection.

- **Striving against odds:** We love a story of struggle, so one way to gain admiration and empathy is to let others know how a brand's source has fought and overcome to get where he is.

- **Defending a worthy cause:** Whether it's saving the environment or fighting for labor rights, associating a Personal Brand with a cause also links the source to the values the cause represents. Deeply politicized causes will alienate those who disagree, while universal causes, like children's literacy, will capture almost everyone.

- **Keeping your word:** It is not flashy, but in a world of relativism—that is, where there are no universal truths, goods or evils and everything depends on your perspective—a person who does what he says he'll do every time is a hero, particularly in business or politics.

- **Rewarding the worthy:** Recognizing those who perform well is a form of self-sacrifice; you are rewarding someone else rather than yourself. Magnanimity and generosity may briefly shine the spotlight on others, but you get the long-term glow.

- **The Golden Rule:** Simply treating others with kindness and respect demands nothing extraordinary, but yields tremendous rewards.

How Goodwill Helps

Goodwill benefits a Personal Brand in more substantial ways than simply provoking a smile when the person's name is brought up. It offers a number of very useful, very powerful advantages:

- **Forgiveness:** We all stumble, but those people whose Personal Brands are weighted with positive feelings are more likely to be given another chance. Contrast self-admitted philanderer Bill Cosby with Michael Jackson. Cosby was forgiven his dalliances with another woman almost overnight; Jackson's longtime allegations of bizarre behavior and improprieties with children blew up in his face in 1993 when he was accused of sexually abusing a young boy. The sick jokes continue to this day, and Jackson's brand is forever stained.

- **Forbearance:** Goodwill often keeps others from leveling criticism because they're willing to wait, watch and see if you can do better. That doesn't mean you're off the hook, but you do have time to set things right.

- **Greater acceptance of sub-par work:** There is no better proof of this concept than Whoopi Goldberg. Despite disastrous projects like the film *Jumpin' Jack Flash* and television's new *Hollywood Squares*, Goldberg has endured to redeem herself with *Ghost* and *Sister Act*. One of the most genial, likable, funny women in entertainment, she has got enough American affection in the bank to see her through many a dry spell.

- **Access:** Who you know begins with who you can get to. Being seen as honorable, honest and principled can open doors that would stay locked for the shifty, shady and untrustworthy.

- **Publicity:** Feel-good stories are like oxygen to editors. Goodwill in a domain vastly improves the chances that a good deed, an award or a milestone will get valuable free coverage. Nobody wants to write about a jerk.

Pitfall: Ulterior Motives

Doing good for good's sake is honored. Doing good for your own gain is reviled, even if the effect is the same. Yes, it's ridiculous, but I didn't make the rules. We love altruism, but we distrust people who benefit from their good deeds, or who camouflage personal agendas in the interest of "the people."

Ex-House Speaker Newt Gingrich's Contract with America and Republican Revolution were touted as a new beginning for ethics, small government and "traditional" American values. But an embarrassing disclosure showed that the moral emperor was naked as a newborn: GOPAC, the non-profit group he had created to further his revolution, had been deeply involved in his college course, Renewing American Civilization, and Gingrich had lied about that fact in ethics hearings needed to get funding for the course. This exposed Gingrich's self-serving agenda, and he later resigned.

Building a Brand as a Complete Jerk

Reader, meet Howard Stern, the repudiation of everything in this chapter. The mega-successful syndicated shock-radio star has built riches and an empire based on a few less-than-endearing qualities: he's vulgar, he's obnoxious, and he treats people like animals, except for women, whom he treats like tramps. Stern proves that you can indeed build a powerful Personal Brand without a shred of goodwill.

But should you? Personal Brands built by projecting negative traits fall into the "you either love him or hate him" category, and creating them takes an unusual person. Building the "bad brand" requires roaring self-confidence, a willingness to offend or alienate many of the people in a domain, and dominant talent that can overcome all the rest. Most of all, it requires a powerful medium to communicate with the domain—to capture their fascination as you revolt them. With his radio and television shows, that's what Stern has done.

Building a brand based on ill will and a bad attitude is tempting. After all, it's a free pass to let loose boorish behavior, uncontrolled ego, and absurd demands. But it is *very* precarious. A person with a "bad" Personal Brand might climb high, but when they fall, no one is there to catch them. The resentment engendered by brutal treatment—and by the fact that the person is a success *despite* being a jerk—leaves the Howard Sterns of the world with a long way to fall.

The heaviest price of this kind of Personal Branding is simple: it's demoralizing. Unless you're the world's most callous jerk, being disliked by 90 percent of the people you work with will get you down. Goodwill is personally energizing.

Obeying the Law of Goodwill

1. **Be true to what you care about:** Authenticity again. Feigning concern over a cause usually results in cries of hypocrisy. In creating

a Personal Brand, stick to what matters on a personal, emotional level, rather than what looks good in a press release.

2. **Stick to the Big Three:** Three personal virtues are universally respected in American culture: *honesty, courage* and *compassion*. Personal Brands that publicly and consistently project at least one of them in a genuine way will score major goodwill points with any domain.

3. **Be visible:** No one will know to feel good about your brand unless they're aware of its admirable qualities. Let people know what about you is worthy of goodwill by sponsoring a charity event, publishing an article about a childhood trial, helping a struggling company on a *pro bono* basis, or something similar.

4. **Be subtle:** We're supposed to tell the world why we're so wonderful, but be subtle about it? Yes, it's possible. You can make your positive qualities visible, but keep quiet about the fact that you're doing so to build your Personal Brand. Some people will guess, others will accuse. Plausibly deny and keep spreading the love.

Personal Brand Profile

Mother Teresa
Modern-Day Saint

It was a measure of the adoration felt for Mother Teresa that upon her death in 1997, devotees immediately began lobbying Rome for her canonization. No human of the century embodied the Christian ideals of compassion, self-sacrifice and care for the needy more strongly than this frail nun from Skopje, Yugoslavia. In a world of Personal Brands built to benefit their sources, hers is the only one built solely on benefiting others.

Mother Teresa (1910-1997)

The woman originally known as Agnes Gonxha Bojaxhiu was born in Skopje, now the capital of Macedonia, on August 27, 1910. Her father, who was of Albanian descent, ran a small farm. At the age of twelve, while attending a Roman Catholic elementary school, she discovered her vocation to help the poor. She decided to train for missionary work, choosing India as the region where she would fulfill her mission.

At eighteen she left her parents' home and joined the Sisters of Loreto, an Irish community of nuns with a mission in Calcutta. After a few months of training in Dublin she was sent to India.

From 1929 to 1948, Mother Teresa taught at St. Mary's High School in Calcutta. But the suffering and poverty she saw outside the convent walls made such a deep impression on her that in 1946 she left the convent school to devote herself to working among the poor in the slums of Calcutta.

How This Brand Was Built

Mother Teresa's Personal Brand arose slowly, over a half-century of work in the horrific slums of Calcutta. From the time she took her vows in 1928, she dedicated herself with extraordinary single-mindedness to aiding the sick and dying of India's cities. In 1950, she founded her order, the Missionaries of Charity, which would formalize her mission to bring relief to those in poor and disaster-stricken corners of the world.

She gained worldwide notoriety by winning the Nobel Peace Prize in 1979, but it was an extraordinary act of self-sacrifice that made her immortal as the "Angel of Calcutta." In 1990, after a nearly fatal heart attack, she announced her intention to resign from her order, and a conclave of sisters was called to choose a successor. In a secret ballot, Mother Teresa was re-elected with only one dissenting vote—her own—and withdrew her request to step down. The willingness to serve even as her own health was failing was an integral part of a great woman's image—an image that inspired millions worldwide.

Why This Brand Works

- **Dedication:** Every culture respects tireless work and dedicated service, and no one epitomized those values more. Her efforts helping the sick and comforting the dying in Calcutta's disease-ridden slums represented years of devotion, faith and a belief that one person could help millions.

- **Higher Goals:** The fact that Mother Teresa was working to save souls, not to improve the public relations picture of a multinational corporation, hugely enhanced her Personal Brand.

- **Modesty:** The diminutive nun never promoted herself or her work, except in those instances when she needed funds or support. This furthered her identity as a selfless healer bent on doing good, not on advertising it. The world was her publicist.

- **Effectiveness:** Mother Teresa made a difference: establishing care centers for the dying, helping alleviate some of the world's direst poverty, and inspiring others to do the same.

Adherence to the Eight Laws

1. **The Law of Specialization.** She was one nun among thousands. Her specialization came from her relentless devotion to helping the poor in one of the world's poorest places.

2. **The Law of Leadership.** Mother Teresa was seen as the symbol of charity, compassion and selfless love for one's fellow man—indeed, the fount of those virtues. Her authority on those topics was absolute.

3. **The Law of Personality.** All her fears, hopes, weaknesses and strengths manifested in her work and her worldwide pleas for aid. Nothing was hidden.

4. **The Law of Distinctiveness.** Mother Teresa's image as the "Saint of Calcutta" was unique in the world. No other cleric this century save the Pope has been so well-known, so celebrated and so connected with a cause or a region.

5. **The Law of Visibility.** One of her strengths was that she did not cultivate visibility for her own sake, but for that of her cause. Her story was compelling, and so she was highly visible, especially as her health declined.

6. **The Law of Unity.** There was really no public or private brand with Mother Teresa; it was all there for everyone to see.

7. **The Law of Persistence.** She embodied the virtues of hard work, sacrifice, and perseverance in the face of enormous odds better than anyone in the twentieth century.

8. **The Law of Goodwill.** Do you know anyone who didn't think Mother Teresa was one of the greatest women in history?

Influence in its Domain

Mother Teresa raised worldwide awareness of the problems in India, and especially in Calcutta. She made it nearly impossible for developed countries to ignore the privation and sickness affecting one-fifth of the Earth's population. Above all, she showed that with politics set aside, the Church could truly be a force for positive change.

Part Three:

How to Build Your
Personal Brand

CHAPTER TWELVE

What's Your Brand?

Determining your current Personal Brand, as well as the effect your brand has on its domain.

You've got the understanding, and you know the rules. Now it's time to put it all together by developing a Personal Brand. Whether you're an individual developing his own brand or a marketing professional working for a company or client, these steps will help you through the four key steps in Personal Branding:

1. Discovering what your current Personal Brand is

2. Creating a new Personal Brand and Personal Brand Statement

3. Putting the new Personal Brand to work

4. Maintaining the Personal Brand

PERSONAL BRAND SELF-TEST

Step 1: What You Project

What aspects of your personality, values system, talents or physical nature are you broadcasting to your domain, consciously or unconsciously? This step establishes a starting point for comparing the message you *think* you send with how others actually perceive you.

Provide one-word or one-phrase answers to these questions:

a. What's the strongest personality characteristic you project to others?

b. What's the value or moral principle others associate with you most?

c. For what ability, skill or talent are you best-known?

d. How would you describe your personal style?

The answers for the first three questions should be things like humor, honesty, or math skills. The answer for number four should be something like extreme, conservative or compassionate. Write down your answers and move to Step Two.

Step 2: What Others Say

This is the difference between what you think you project and what others think of you. For this exercise, select five to eight people who know you well and whom you can trust to be completely candid. This takes a thick skin; you may find out things you wish you hadn't. But if you're going to build a great Personal Brand, grit your teeth and proceed.

Ask your participants for one-word or one-phrase answers to the following questions. Give them the questions in writing and time to think about them for twenty-four hours or so, but give them a deadline.

a. What do you see as the dominant aspect of my personality?

b. What moral principle or value do you most closely associate with me?

c. What skill, ability or talent comes to mind when you think of me?

d. How do you describe me to others who've never met me?

The answers here may be a bit more nebulous, because you can't control what others say. Hold them to the one word or one phrase rule, but otherwise let them be. Get your answers and move to Step Three.

Step 3: Your Effect on Others

The truest test of your Personal Brand is what effect it has on people, situations and decision-making when you're not around. But short of hiring a spy to scope out family gatherings or company meetings, you've got no direct way to gather such data. So we'll rely on the next best thing: how others react when they first meet you.

For this exercise:

a. Dig into your memory of meeting new people—those to whom you've been introduced and who have some background information on you, and those whom you meet "cold," with no introduction.

b. Carefully observe and catalog your meetings with new people over the next few weeks.

With your encounters in mind, produce one-word or one-phrase answers to these questions:

a. How do acquaintances most commonly introduce you to a stranger?

b. In subsequent conversation, what topic will the stranger most often steer towards, especially in asking questions?

c. People you meet "cold" will usually develop a near-instant, gut-level feeling toward you. In your case, how intense is that feeling? Whether it's affinity or dislike doesn't matter; rate it on a 1-10 scale, with 1 being "apathetic" and 10 being "ultra-powerful."

Step 4: Plotting the Balance

Get a piece of paper and write your Step One results side by side in a row, then do the same for one set of Step Two results, placing the Step Two row below Step One with six inches or so in between. Now you have four columns with your established extremes:

	Personality	Principle	Talent	Personality Style
	Confidence	Honesty	Speed	Edgy
YOU				
OTHERS				
	Wit	Directness	Creativity	Temperamental

a. Look at the words at either end of each column. How closely do they match? Did you think your strongest personality trait was confidence, but an interviewee said it was hyperactivity? You have an imbalance, but you won't know its extent until you plot all your responses.

b. Go through the answers to all four questions in both steps. Plot each person's word or phrase in the appropriate column; the more it differs from your own response, the farther down the column it goes, even if it's below the first answer you plotted. For example, if your answer to question number two was *kindness* but a friend's was *ruthlessness*, that goes far down the page. Once you're done, you'll have a page that looks like this:

	Personality	Principle	Talent	Personality Style
	Confidence	Honesty	Speed	Edgy
YOU	Confidence	Openness	Meet Deadlines	Informal
	Arrogance	Responsibility		Outside-the-box
			Leadership	Creative
		Candor		
	Caring	Reliability	Brainstorming	
	Intelligence		Big Ideas	Weird
OTHERS	Humor	Compassion	Writing	Obnoxious
	Wit	Directness	Creativity	Temperamental

c. Take a look at your four columns. How much space is between your Step One answers and others' Step Two responses? If most of the responses are far away, there's an imbalance between what you think you're projecting and others' perception of you. If they're bunched, you're being seen as you intend to. For most people, the result is somewhere in between.

d. Finally, find the three middle responses for each column. Write them down separately. Now hit the thesaurus, dictionary or local English professor and find a single word or phrase that summarizes all three. For example: if the three middle words were *competitive-*

ness, fairness and *ambition*, distill that down to *"driven but ethical."* You should end up with four such phrases, often with "but" or "and" in the middle. What you've got is a rough but clear point of equilibrium between how you are trying to *be* perceived and how you really *are* perceived.

I	Personality	Principle	Talent	Personality Style
	Confidence	Honesty	Speed	Edgy
	Arrogance	Responsibility	Leadership	Outside-the-box
	Caring	Candor	Brainstorming	Creative
	Intelligence	Reliability	Big Ideas	Weird

II **Personality:** "Kindly Brilliant"

Principle: "Dependable and Frank"

Talent: "Creative Trailblazing"

Personality Style: "Utterly Original"

Is such inexact information really useful? Yes, because it reflects the true nature of perception. No one will ever perceive you as an absolute, and since we're looking for the perceptions of many people, the results will be indistinct. We're looking for a signpost, not an "X."

Step 5: Calculating Your Effect

Now look at what you wrote for Step Three.

a. Summarize how people introduce you in four words or less.

b. Choose the most common topic of questioning.

c. Figure the average intensity of feeling on the 1-10 scale.

Your results should look something like this:

a. "Talented, funny writer"

b. My reviews

c. 7.6

This information tells you what aspects of your Personal Brand are retaining their effect in your absence, what people are telling others about you, and how strong a feeling the Personal Brand attributes you project are evoking.

Step 6: Your Perception Set

Take all four summaries from Step Four, and turn them into a single sentence. For example, these were your results:

Question 1: "intense but humorous"

Question 2: "driven but ethical"

Question 3: "organized writer"

Question 4: "speaks his mind"

The resulting sentence would read: "A funny, honest, organized writer with a sharp tongue and a fire in his belly." This is your perception set.

Step 7: Your Domain Effect

Now take those three results from Step Five and write an analysis of how you are affecting your domain based on that information. For example: "My writing talent stands out, but so does my concern for professional recognition. The attributes I project have a moderately strong effect on my audience." This is your domain effect.

Perception Set + Domain Effect = Personal Brand

Accident or Not?

Now that you've worked through the self-test, you should have a clearer picture of your Personal Brand. But, is that brand intentional or unintentional? Are you where you are because of some strategy, or is it completely by accident?

If your Personal Brand is accidental, you're in the majority. As I said in the beginning, most people are neither aware of spontaneous branding, nor would they know how to identify their brand if they knew they had one. Having an unintentional Personal Brand puts you in a pretty good position, because you have no bad habits to break. You can simply begin developing your new Personal Brand.

However, if your current brand is the result of a plan, is it the Personal Brand you want? If not, what have you done to establish a brand identity that's not serving your goals? Take a close look at your behavior, your professional persona, marketing methods— anything that may have contributed to your off-target brand. Once you identify what you've done, stop it. *Immediately.* Your goal is to have a clean slate, and that can only occur when you've quit counterproductive behavior.

How Your Current Brand Affects You

Just as you may not have realized what your Personal Brand is, you may not have known how it has been affecting your life. Nothing is more important—Personal Branding is about *taking control* of how people's perceptions affect you. Three main ways your Personal Brand impacts your life and work:

- **Expectations:** People in your personal and professional life set their expectations based on their perception of your ability, your attitude and your values. They also decide ahead of time how to react if you don't meet those expectations.

- **Opportunities:** Whether or not you even get a chance at a job, a client or a promotion depends on whether you're in the decision set. Perception has as much to do with getting an interview or a chance to pitch as ability and experience.

- **Rewards:** Like opportunities, rewards are often predetermined by presumption of worthiness. A baseball player might win the Most Valuable Player award for his league based largely on playing with a winning team in a major market, while a player with better statistics who plays on a small market team goes unnoticed.

The Right Brand at the Right Time

So now you know how the world has branded you. Is this the Personal Brand you want and deserve? Even if the answer is no, it may not be the right time for you to create a new one. You may be in a time of personal or professional transition, or you may already be so busy that you couldn't handle the opportunity a stronger brand would bring. All I suggest is that after discovering your current Personal Brand, ask these three questions:

1. In my domain, what goals mean the most to me?

2. Is my Personal Brand helping or hurting my attainment of those goals?

3. Does it affect my feelings of happiness and satisfaction in either a positive or negative way?

Depending on the answers, you'll know whether or not it's time to look at launching a re-born Personal Brand.

When You Should Develop a New Personal Brand

- **When you feel unrecognized for accomplishments:** Mediocre work by big names often draws more attention than great work by the obscure. Why? Brand identity. If you feel passed over, make them take notice.

- **When others are achieving the goals you set for yourself:** There's nothing more bitter than saying, "That should have been me." Look at your most cherished goals; you will probably see ways Personal Branding can help you achieve them more quickly than you realized.

- **When you feel you have gone as far as you can conventionally:** You've been working long hours, improving your skills, meeting the right people… and still you're climbing the ladder at a snail's pace. Personal Branding is revolutionary enough that you might be the only one in your domain doing it, making it a great tool for creating your own shortcuts.

- **When you want an edge over the competition:** They're as good as you. They're as connected as you are. But do they have an image as precise and powerful as yours? In the battle against competitors, a great Personal Brand is an atomic bomb.

Personal Brand Profile

Carl Sagan
The People's Scientist

If you've ever heard of Search for Extra-Terrestrial Intelligence (SETI) black holes or the phrase "billions and billions" (which he never said), thank Carl Sagan. The late astronomer, who died in 1996, remains the popular face of cosmology and space science for millions of Americans: a kindly, unfailingly humanistic voice speaking out against superstition and global pollution and in favor of exploration and the popularization of scientific knowledge. No one did as much to give science a human face.

Carl Sagan (1934-1996)

Born in Brooklyn, Sagan first found himself captivated by the stars when, in a library book, he learned that the tiny, twinkling points of light were in fact mighty suns made small by their incredible distance from Earth. This fascination fueled Sagan's stunning academic career, as he entered the University of Chicago in 1951 at age sixteen, earned a bachelor's degree in liberal arts in 1954 and in physics in 1955, a master's in physics in 1956, and his Ph.D. in astronomy and astrophysics in 1960.

Astronomy at the time was in love with the stars. Planets were seen with suspicion after a study had produced an embarrassment of false claims about Martian canals early in the century. Deeply curious about extraterrestrial life, Sagan pursued the topic enthusiastically, but skeptically, citing a favorite credo, "extraordinary claims require extraordinary evidence."

Sagan took aim at presumptions of plant life on Mars, coordinated seventy of the world's top scientists in a radio telescope search for alien life that would become SETI (Search for Extraterrestrial Intelligence), and in 1968, assumed a post at Cornell University. There, he would spend the rest of his life writing and encouraging discovery.

How This Brand Was Built

Sagan's Personal Brand was built by television—more specifically, by the landmark PBS series *Cosmos*, which debuted in 1980 and has now been seen by more than 500 million viewers. This thirteen-part series took viewers on a journey through a myriad of scientific topics from cell biology to global warming to the possible end of the universe—each step led by Sagan in a role that was part bard, part teacher and part post-Einstein scholar. *Cosmos* cast Sagan in the role of populist scientist, and made him the voice outside the ivory tower.

The other half of Sagan's brand was based on his scientific successes. Indeed, his credibility as the creator of *Cosmos* and the media personality he later became would not have been possible had he not established himself as a preeminent author, theorist and specialist in exobiology, the speculative science dealing with life on other worlds. In his work with such groundbreaking missions as Mariner, Viking, Voyager and Pathfinder, Sagan solidified his place as a multidisciplinary space scientist.

Why This Brand Works

• **Expertise:** Whatever his colleagues might have thought of him for having the temerity to "popularize science," Sagan was an illustrious theoretician and applied scientist who advanced theories about planetary environments that were unique for their time. In his fields, he was seen as the authority.

- **Values:** Sagan's ongoing mission was to open the world's eyes to the dangers of fundamentalism, superstition, environmental degradation, and shortsightedness. In other words, he advocated causes almost anyone could support.

- **Audience Respect:** He knew his audience well, and he likewise knew that if cosmological and biological principles were lowered from their holy heights and made clear to the people, the people would understand and respond. And they did.

- **Fascination:** Sagan talked about some very cool stuff: black holes, faster-than-light travel, the potential for life on Mars, World War III, and a lot more. And he made it easy to understand.

Adherence to the Eight Laws

1. **The Law of Specialization.** No other scientist left the ivy-covered labs to talk directly to the people. Sagan did it without being condescending or obtuse, and his identity became unique.

2. **The Law of Leadership.** Though he earned the enmity of some colleagues who saw him as a self-promoter, the public perceived him as what he was: a leading space scientist with a vast library of knowledge.

3. **The Law of Personality.** Sagan's quirky manner and boyish enthusiasm in more than thirty appearances on *The Tonight Show* were completely genuine.

4. **The Law of Distinctiveness.** From his *Cosmos*-era turtlenecks to his speaking timbre that led to the famous "billions and billions" attribution, he developed a truly unique public persona.

5. **The Law of Visibility.** Sagan published more than thirty books, won a Pulitzer Prize, created *Cosmos* and consistently appeared on a huge

range of television shows. He *was* the voice of science and rationality for Americans.

6. **The Law of Unity.** If there was a self-promotional or false side to Sagan, as some of his peers liked to claim, it never became public knowledge. His public and private selves appeared balanced.

7. **The Law of Persistence.** Until a few months before his death, he continued writing, producing, advising on space missions designed to explore the solar system for signs of life, and so on. His enthusiasm never flagged.

8. **The Law of Goodwill.** Warm, funny and engaging, Sagan made science comprehensible—and made people feel smarter. They loved him for it.

Influence in its Domain

Carl Sagan brought science into the domain where it truly belongs: the lives and minds of the people whose tax dollars pay most of the bills. His efforts to popularize scientific methods and principles paved the way for physicists like Stephen Hawking, and created a wider awareness of the fragile nature of the planet Earth.

CHAPTER THIRTEEN

Creating a New Personal Brand

A step-by-step guide to crafting a new Personal Brand, with the Personal Brand Statement at its core.

Now you know where you stand. The next step is to craft a Personal Brand that is in line with your goals. But, the question remains: can you re-brand a person?

The Persistence of Branding

In a word, yes. But it is incredibly difficult, and the degree of difficulty varies with the level to which the old brand is etched on the minds of the audience.

There is a physiological reason for this. Repeated exposure to an experience stimulates the same neural pathways in the brain, over and over, until the neurons automatically fire and create the same sensation whenever that stimulus is encountered—like wearing a track in a carpet by walking down the same path for years. That's why people repeat behaviors, even when they know they're not healthy: the reactions are hard-wired into our cerebral cortexes. In the same way, when people encounter you, your current Personal Brand affects them, without any effort from you or them.

The longer and more intense the exposure, the more time and work required to change your brand identity.

How to Bury an Ingrained Personal Brand

Birthing a shiny new Personal Brand is only half the battle. You've also got to drive a stake through the heart of the old one. Not everything about you that went into your current brand should be thrown away; those things that are the "real" you should also be in the new brand. But you're going to re-package some characteristics and promote new ones, and that means burning the old packaging.

The only way to do it is by consistently promoting and developing a new Personal Brand and letting nature take its course. If you're dealing with the same domain, only time and a boldly realized, distinctive, clear new Personal Brand will make people drop the perceptual baggage they associate with you.

Four Powerful Ways to Change a Brand

• **Change your domain:** Get into a different field. This isn't an option for many people, but if it is, it's a great way to clean the slate and start fresh. For example, a political lobbyist with negative baggage could go into private law practice.

• **Change your location:** You can stay in the same domain, but just set up shop in a different place. Again, this may not be an option, or your domain may be so close-knit that changing addresses makes no difference. But it offers possibilities.

• **Public rehabilitation:** This is a rough one, but if you're desperate... Basically, this involves standing before your audience and doing a *mea culpa*, taking the heat for past mistakes, baring your soul and vowing to change everything. It doesn't always work, and it's hard on the ego. But, as we saw with Drew Barrymore, it can work.

• **Time passing:** Get out of your domain for awhile and let memories fade. Legendary film director Elia Kazan did this after cooperating with the McCarthy hearings in the 1950s; upon receiving a Lifetime Achievement Academy Award in 2000, he had gone from hated turncoat to sympathetic artist.

Key Personal Brand Components

- **Emotional impact:** Your brand must connect with your audience on an emotional level, not just an intellectual or benefit level. Decisions are made based on feelings of affinity, comfort or confidence as much as they are based on fact and reason.

- **Focus:** Orient your brand on a single service, field of expertise, product or talent, within a single domain. People like to work with specialists.

- **Clarity:** The message your brand sends—what you do, how well you do it, who you do it for, how good you are at it—must be completely unambiguous.

- **Non-neutrality:** Weight your brand with a sense of character and personality, instead of being safe and middle-of-the-road. It can be funny, edgy, hyper, combative…just so long as it's not boring.

- **Accomplishment:** Develop your brand around skill, experience and recognition. Pick an area of expertise in which you surpass 95 percent of others in your domain. People might select you based on emotion, but longevity depends on whether you can provide a service they need, and do it well.

- **Truth:** There must be truth behind your brand; it should reflect who you are, what you care about, where your passions lie, and what you're best at.

- **Enthusiasm:** Finally, don't build a brand that doesn't fire your passions. You won't be able to keep building it. Pursue something you can get excited about.

EIGHT STEPS TO
CREATING A NEW PERSONAL BRAND*

Step 1: Select Your Goals

What do you want to accomplish with your Personal Brand? Recognition? Advancement? Increased business? Divide your goals up based on Term and Type:

Term

- *Short-term goals*—Can be realized within six months to a year after your Personal Brand launch.

- *Mid-term goals*—Can be realized in one to three years after your launch.

- *Long-term goals*—Major goals set three years or more after brand launch.

Type

- *Material goals*—How much money do you want to make? How big do you want your company to grow? Where do you want to live, etc.?

- *Position goals*—These are about status and authority: the job you'd like, the promotion you want, your respect in your profession, etc.

- *Personal goals*—What do you want to get from achieving your Material and Position goals? Freedom? Respect? Wealth? To do what you love? Power? To help others?

---

*For more ideas on how to craft and maintain a Personal Brand visit www.petermontoya.com or call (866) 288-9300.

Step 2: Research the Competition

Knowing whom you're competing with in your domain does more than let you know who to watch out for—it gives you priceless tactical and strategic information. Answer the following questions:

a. Who are your key competitors?

b. How long has each been in your domain?

c. How is each positioned?

d. What are each one's strengths?

e. What are each one's weaknesses?

f. How can you leverage those weaknesses to your advantage?

g. What need of your domain is no competitor meeting, and can you meet it?

h. Would alliance with any of them be to your advantage?

Create a brief profile of each key competitor (see the following page). As you do, you'll start to see common themes and weaknesses.

Competitor Profile	
Name:	Tom K.
Job:	Business Development
Time in Domain:	7 years
Positioned as:	Brown-noser
Strengths:	Networking, Sales, Social Situations
Weakness:	No real accomplishments, dishonest, doesn't know technology
Advantages:	Lack of tech knowledge and ideas allows me to stand out and present bold new ideas
Unmet needs:	New thinking, candor with upper management
Action:	Develop aggressive new 2002 plan

Some of the best ways to do competitive research:

• Talk to your competitors' colleagues under the guise of being a potential client and ask for an assessment

• Talk to your competitors' clients in the same manner and get their candid assessment

• Read and study industry trade publications

• Scour your competitors' Web sites

• Interview competitors directly

Step 3: Evaluate Yourself

What are your strongest areas? Do they benefit your domain? Have you overestimated your abilities in one area and underestimated them in another? Is your personality suited to your domain's culture? List:

a. Your areas of greatest skill, talent or knowledge

b. Your most glaring weaknesses

c. Your greatest areas of professional interest or passion

d. Your dominant personality traits

e. Your personal style—how you approach your work, how you behave toward others

It's a tall order, but since success rests on the ability to create a Personal Brand that reflects the *whole person*, it is a necessary process.

Step 4: Know Your Domain

• You've got to know your domain's culture and people intimately.

• What is your domain?

• How would you characterize the domain's culture? (casual, wild, conservative, etc.)

• What qualities does it value most (knowledge, speed, appearance, etc.)?

• What are its greatest needs?

• Is there a "lingo" or specialized knowledge that carries status (computer programming, for example)?

- Who are the centers of influence—organizations and individuals?

- What media and communications channels dominate?

- How are people promoting themselves?

- What psychological factors motivate decision-making?

- Do you already have possible allies within the domain?

Get inside the minds of the people in your target market. Find out what makes them tick, why they make decisions, who they choose to favor and who they discard. Get every kernel of psychological information you can and save it.

Step 5: Write Your Personal Branding Statement

The Personal Branding Statement, or PBS, clearly, concisely expresses the core components of your brand:

a. Who you are (your specialty)

b. What you do (your service)

c. To whom are your services directed?

d. Your leading attribute

Examples:

- Jack Nicholson—"An acerbic, brilliantly talented actor of dangerously intense character who revels in his caustic, Lakers-obsessed Hollywood image."

- Stephen King—"A nerdy, funny New Englander who's turned a childhood interest in horror and a gift for storytelling into his place as the world's bestselling author."

- Alan Greenspan—"A gruff, unemotional Fed chairman and economist who guides the economy with a firm hand and a watchful eye on inflation."

Complete the following exercises to create your PBS:

PBS Exercise PBS Exercise 1: Determine Who You Are

a. Look at the Step 3 list (Evaluate Yourself). Write down your three greatest professional skills or abilities.

b. Look at the Step 4 list (Know Your Domain). Write down the three greatest needs of your domain.

c. Combine your skills and abilities into a single idea. Example: if your three skills are illustrator, photographer and designer, combine them as "visual artist." This is your skill set.

d. Look at your domain's greatest need and adjust the description of your skill set to fit. Example: if your domain needs old-fashioned architectural illustration, change "visual artist" to "pen and pencil renderer." You're not changing your skills, merely how they're packaged.

This is your specialty, a skill set matched to the needs of the audience. This is *who you are*.

PBS Exercise 2: Determine What You Do

a. Look at the Step 3 "Evaluate Yourself" list and write down your greatest area of professional interest. This reflects the kind of work you wish to pursue, not necessarily what you're doing now.

b. Define your area of interest as it applies to the service you provide. For example, your goal is conceptual design and your service is rendering for the architectural industry. Your statement would be

"Cutting-edge concepts for twenty-first century architectural design." This is *what you do.*

At the start, you may not be able to jump right into your area of great interest. But you can still state your end goal in your PBS. This allows you to build your image gradually while using the PBS as a reminder of your ultimate objective.

PBS Exercise 3: Determine Your Leading Attribute

a. Look at the Step 3 "Evaluate Yourself" list. Write down your three dominant personality traits and the three key aspects of your personal style.

b. Look at the Step 4 "Know Your Domain" list. List the three biggest aspects of your domain's culture and the three qualities it values most. You should end up with something like this:

- Dominant personality traits: charisma, impulsiveness, intelligence

- Personal style: irreverent, hyperactive, loves surfwear

- Domain culture: high-pressure, creative, businesslike

- Valued qualities: attention to detail, "outside the box" thinking, candor

c. Write a capsule description of your domain based on the "domain culture" and "valued qualities." Using the example above, it would be "Creatively intense."

d. Now look at "dominant personality traits" and "personal style." Which responses fit your domain best? In this case, it's intelligence and hyperactivity, perfect for a fast-paced, creative environment.

e. Now, express those two characteristics—intelligence and hyperactivity—in a single, more descriptive phrase, like "high-velocity thinking." That's your *leading attribute*, the guideline you'll use to help your audience form the right perceptions about you.

PBS Exercise 4: Add Your Domain and Write

The Personal Branding Statement equation looks like this:

Specialty + Service + Leading Attribute + Domain = PBS

You've picked your domain, so add it to the equation and write the whole thing out, changing the order of elements if necessary. This isn't a slogan so don't worry about length or cleverness. What matters is clarity and completeness. Following the formula, the PBS for our fictional artist would be:

"A skilled pen and pencil renderer providing high-velocity conceptual thinking for the cutting-edge experimental architecture community."

Step 6: Create Your Message

Once you have your Personal Branding Statement, craft the message that will carry your brand to your domain. The message is not the exact words you write or images you use, but the essence of what you want to say about your skills, your personality and your leading attribute.

Your message should have the following components:

• What you do

• How you do it—your style, your speed, etc.

• How it benefits others

- Something to produce an emotional reaction—humor, sarcasm, etc.

Step 7: Propagate Your Message

Get the word out to your domain by all the means you can afford, and as consistently as possible. Methods include:

- **Advertising:** Placing print ads in a trade publication, running banner ads on a trade Web site, taking exhibit space at an industry conference, and so on.

- **Publicity:** Sending press releases to generate press coverage about your new Web site, an award you've received, some philanthropic cause you're working for on the side, etc. You can also get yourself into editors' Rolodexes as a quotable source for your area of expertise.

- **Publishing:** Writing for industry magazines, newsletters, Web sites, the appropriate section of local newspapers, and so on. Publishing a book is even better, and is an excellent long-term goal.

- **Networking:** One of the strongest ways to get your message out. Attending industry functions, networking groups, serving on professional panels, joining advocacy groups, unions and the like.

- **Internet:** Putting up your own Web site is virtually mandatory these days. But beyond that, you can participate in online seminars, act as a topic-oriented guide for sites like About.com, and circulate your name on specialty bulletin boards and discussion groups.

- **Word of mouth:** Let your skill do the talking by doing great work, handing out some business cards so people know who's responsible, and disappearing. People talk, and organic buzz usually follows.

Step 8: Live Your Brand

Everything is in place, now you need to be able to back it up. Work your Personal Brand—the promises it makes, the personality and habits that underpin it, the talents you promote—into every aspect of your life in some way. The ways can be subtle—you don't need to change the way you dress or eat—but weaving your brand into your lifestyle makes it easier to maintain.

Schedule, Schedule

The final step in birthing your new Personal Brand is managing time. Though the effects of your brand can be unpredictable, this is not a random process; it must be managed. Create a master Personal Brand Schedule.

Your Schedule will chart every aspect of your Personal Brand development process—what you do, when you do it, how you follow up, and so on. It should include:

- Dates for mailing materials

- Dates for completing new promotional materials such as business cards

- Dates for events such as conferences

- Times to spend analyzing your brand's effects and making adjustments

- Milestones—what you want to achieve by a given time: promotions, income figures, increases in market share, and so on. These are very useful signposts for how your Personal Brand is doing.

Tom Hanks
The Everyman

Tom Hanks is a marvelous example of a person gradually evolving his Personal Brand over time through smart decision making and great performance, not hype. In his journey from television comedian to film comedian to Oscar-winning leading man, he has emerged as one of the truly beloved American stars: a box office power who's regarded as an accessible, likable Everyman.

Tom Hanks (1956 –   )

Born in the East Bay city of Concord, California, Hanks was raised by his father, Amos, a chef, along with his brother and sister. The family moved frequently, and by the time Hanks had reached high school age had settled in Oakland, where he attended school and was bitten by the theater bug after watching a staging of Eugene O'Neill's *The Iceman Cometh*.

Refining his craft in theater, in several short-lived sitcoms and in a few poorly received films, Hanks came to public attention in the Penny Marshall film *Big*, about a thirteen-year-old boy transplanted into the body of a man. This film earned Hanks his first Oscar nomination for Best Actor, and set him on course to become the Jimmy Stewart of his generation.

How This Brand Was Built

Hanks followed a common path: he caught the theater bug during his college days in Northern California, and followed with years of stage roles and backstage work, learning his craft. As a result, when he appeared in the sitcom *Bosom Buddies* in 1980, his performance was memorable and affecting, even though the show did not endure. Hanks had done the grunt work necessary to hone his craft, and it earned him the notice of directors like Ron Howard.

Hanks has also developed his career with great intelligence and shrewdness. When he was in danger of being typecast as the wacky lead in teenage movies like *Bachelor Party* and *Splash*, he surprised everyone with *Big*. And when he appeared to be specializing in light-hearted summer films, along came the riveting *Philadelphia*, for which he earned his first Oscar. Hanks has constantly worked to grow as an artist, seeking new challenges and never getting stale.

His other key building block: his Jimmy Stewart accessibility. Hanks has chosen roles that allow his good guy qualities to shine through—or he has brought those qualities out in lesser roles. He's the common man's superstar.

Why This Brand Works

• **Talent:** Hanks has a world of talent, without question. The muse spoke to him in college, and he was smart enough to listen.

• **Patience:** Unlike too many young performers who try to use good looks or connections to short-circuit the process of learning the actor's craft, Hanks learned the classics, spent time in regional theater, and developed his chops over years of work. He's smart enough to know that when a trend passes, all the actor has to fall back on is his skill.

• **Alliances:** Ron Howard, Steven Spielberg, Robert Zemeckis—Hanks has chosen to work with some of the most successful directors in Hollywood, and the results have been some of his biggest triumphs. He's picked his partners well.

• **Risk:** From *From the Earth to the Moon* to *That Thing You Do!*, Hanks has never shied from risky projects. Rather than taking a page from the Brando handbook and taking a role once a decade, he gets out there and tries new things, which adds to his appeal.

Adherence to the Eight Laws

1. **The Law of Specialization.** There are plenty of actors. But leading men who specialize in gentle humor and poignant heroism? There aren't many like Hanks.

2. **The Law of Leadership.** Winner of two Oscars and a nominee several times more, he's acknowledged as one of the finest actors working today, as well as one of Hollywood's top five box office attractions.

3. **The Law of Personality.** Nothing about Hanks appears contrived or glitzy, including his none-to-overwhelming looks. He seems like a regular guy who just happened to find a script one day.

4. **The Law of Distinctiveness.** Hanks' distinctiveness is expressed in his film work, and it is like no other leading man's: thoughtful, textured, and effortlessly human.

5. **The Law of Visibility.** His consistent output of high profile projects ensures that at least once a year, there's a Tom Hanks performance being called "the best performance of the year."

6. **The Law of Unity.** Behind the scenes, he's a committed family man married to actress Rita Wilson, and "that's all I have to say about that," as one of Hanks' famous characters said.

7. **The Law of Persistence.** As mentioned earlier, Hanks did his time in regional plays, making guest appearances on sitcoms and doing dog films like The *Money Pit* before breaking out as a superstar.

8. **The Law of Goodwill.** Almost everyone adores Hanks: critics, women, blue-collar men, intellectuals, his peers. He's accessible,

genial and normal—one of us instead of a member of the Hollywood jet set.

Influence in its Domain

Tom Hanks certainly wields influence over the current movie industry—his star power can get a film made or killed with a phone call. Beyond that arena, he's made the landscape safe for non-hunks with stunning acting skills—the Edward Nortons of the world—to take their place at the top of the Hollywood pantheon.

CHAPTER FOURTEEN

Putting Your Personal Brand to Work

Leveraging a new Personal Brand for maximum strategic advantage.

There's a line in a song by Jimmy Buffett that says, "Relationships. We've all got 'em. We all want 'em. What do we do with 'em?" The same can apply to creating a Personal Brand—you've built it, now what do you do with it? This chapter is dedicated to helping you figure that out.

What Can a Personal Brand Do?

The potential for a strong Personal Brand is really limited only by the imagination and skill of the person controlling it, whether that's an individual or a marketing professional. Some of the most common possibilities for a Personal Brand:

• **Advancement:** Your brand can put you into consideration for a higher position or higher status within a community of peers. This occurs when the brand elevates your standing by repeated exposure, the old "If I keep seeing it, it must be good" dynamic.

• **Money:** By increasing the perception that you are in demand, and by making your strengths more obvious, your brand puts you in a position of negotiating strength. A good Personal Brand transforms you from a commodity to someone unique, with unique benefits. That translates to higher compensation.

- **Respect:** One of the best uses for a Personal Brand is letting your domain know about the quality of your work and the level of your expertise. Your brand will not earn you respect, but its power can help publicize your strongest work or your skill. Ultimately, people respect those who do the job or have the tools.

- **Entrepreneurship:** A Personal Brand is not just invaluable in building a small business, but in starting and developing one. If you are an aspiring entrepreneur, a great brand can help you raise money, get credit, take customers from competitors, and differentiate yourself from the herd.

- **Access:** This may be the most powerful way to use your brand. Strong brand identities with high visibility create an aura that makes others feel or assume the person behind the brand is worth talking to. You can leverage this fact to get access to people of influence.

Tactical Brand Benefits

We've learned about the general benefits of having a Personal Brand. Now it's time to move on to the tactical benefits, the ones that can actually affect your day-to-day success.

- **Credibility:** A brand that suggests knowledge or talent gives your words and deeds much higher credibility. Practically, this translates to: clients believing you when you cite what a project will require; your opinion being taken when you assess a person's skills; and you being more likely to be trusted with valuable business. You become a "center of trust," which can mean greater opportunity.

- **Second Look:** Getting a second look can mean you are given greater consideration for an opportunity than others who are not well branded. It can also mean your work is given more of a chance to impress others, or that people look harder to find something worthwhile in your work. Basically, it gets you the benefit of the doubt.

- **Magnetism:** Celebrities' magnetism often comes from their Personal Brand, from its air of mystery, style or sex appeal. Your brand can do the same, creating magnetism, the feeling that you are worth meeting and worth getting to know. Imagine the possibilities if you attracted opportunities instead of chasing them.

- **Intimidation:** When it comes to the competition, this is war. A great Personal Brand leads to a reputation that can intimidate competitors right out of your way. Some presume that your skills are superior to theirs, and they create excessive pressure for themselves. Others assume you have the inside track on the business and never even compete for it. Either way, intimidation thins the herd.

Leveraging Your Personal Brand - The Workplace

The workplace might be a corporate office, a design studio, a movie set or a courtroom. No matter what it is, a powerful Personal Brand is an advantage. Being known for certain traits and skills in a small domain ensures that your brand is known and people are familiar with what you stand for. This gives you the ability to control their expectations and decisions. For example:

- Getting a greater or a lesser role in a project

- Inspiring others to work harder under your leadership

- Getting an unusual idea heard and acted upon

- Exceeding expectations you've set, thereby elevating your status

- Getting the greater share of credit for a group project in the mind of a superior

- Convincing an audience you're right

Leveraging Your Personal Brand – Your Profession

Broadening the scope of the domain a bit, we come to your line of work—actor, consultant, computer programmer, photographer. Here, you have a wider audience to work on, but a tougher task in influencing them, because there are more brands and more messages. In this realm, your Personal Brand has one main goal: building your reputation. It can also help you:

- Create a buzz about your skills or your personality

- Turn that buzz into referral business, testimonials and recommendations

- Gain visibility with industry press and editors

- Gain greater notice of your work

- Clarify what you do

- Differentiate yourself to potential future customers or employers

- Imply that you're superior to your colleagues

Leveraging Your Personal Brand with Your Personal Life*

Your Personal Brand will spill over into your personal life; there's no avoiding it. You have two choices: embrace the spillover and make a little of your professional brand part of your private persona, or resist it. Like it or not, there are ways your Personal Brand can benefit you in your non-working life. Your Personal Brand can:

- Make you stand out to others

- Create awareness of and respect for your profession

---

*For the Special Report "Leveraging Your Everyday Personal Brand," visit www.petermontoya.com, or call (866) 288-9300 and we'll fax it to you.

- Communicate your professional passion to friends and family

- Create interest in you and your work

What Your Personal Brand Should NOT Do

- **Change your personality:** Your brand should be built on your true personality and character. Changing your personality to fit a brand is as much a lie as building a brand based on fabrication. It will damage your professional fortunes and make people view you as a fraud.

- **Make enemies:** It's one thing to beat out a competitor for business. It's quite another to humiliate, taunt or embarrass a competitor to the point where he aches to ruin you. You can compete without confrontation; your Personal Brand identity should be confident without being cocky, and should attempt to praise or assist competitors...before leaving them bleeding in the dust.

- **Negatively affect your personal life:** Losing friends, lovers or family because of your Personal Brand is too high a price for success. If such things are happening, ask yourself if your brand offends someone, makes you appear arrogant or ungrateful, or if your success has simply robbed you of time with the people you care about. This is a whole-life approach to having a great Personal Brand; you need the whole life to make it work.

Personal Brand Profile

Tiger Woods
The Greatest Golfer in the World

We began with Tiger Woods, and with good reason: his Personal Brand stands out as perhaps the most dominant of the current era. Why? A simple reason: he intimidates his fellow golfers just with his presence. If Woods shows up at a tournament, everyone else is presumed to be playing for second place. That's absurd, of course; the man's only human. But his proven excellence and reputation for savage competitiveness give Woods an edge before he steps to the first tee.

Tiger Woods [1975 –   ]

Eldrick Woods was born Orlando, Florida. Early on, his parents, Earl (a retired Army lieutenant) and Kultilda Woods (a native of Thailand), introduced their only child to the sport he has come to dominate, giving him a sawed-off putter to practice with as soon as he could stand up on his own.

His skill at the game manifested early, when at age three, he shot a 48 for nine holes at the Navy Golf Club in Cypress, California. By age five, the young prodigy had been featured in *Golf Digest* and appeared on the TV program *That's Incredible*. By the time he won the first of six Optimist International Junior World Titles at age eight, it was clear this was no ordinary talent.

How This Brand Was Built

Woods's fame is a direct product of arguably the most stellar career in amateur and professional sports. Starting when he was fifteen years old, he won three straight United States Junior Championships (1991-1993) and three straight United States Amateur Championships (1994-1996). From there it was off to Stanford and the NCAA title, then turning pro in 1996 as perhaps the most celebrated ex-amateur of all time. Four consecutive Majors later, he's seen by many as the greatest golfer ever—at age twenty-seven.

But Woods's Personal Brand is also the product of fortunate timing—between a gifted, charismatic young man and a golf industry trying to appeal to and sell to an untapped demographic:

American youth. Woods became the perfect vehicle for that pitch, leading even more to his high visibility, famed endorsements, and growing wealth.

Why This Brand Works

- **Results:** Woods is the best golfer in the world. His feats so far leave longtime observers of the game in awe, and wondering what he could possibly do better.

- **Charm:** With his smile, his energy on the course and his personality, Woods serves as a winning contrast to the majority of staid, controlled professional golfers. His charm is one reason behind his enormous success as a spokesman.

- **Fascination:** Everyone wants to watch the best in action, to see for themselves the subtle movements that separate genius from just another hack. We can't get enough of watching this young man strike a white ball.

- **Uniqueness:** Very simply, Woods is a young ethnic (African American, Thai and Native American) in a sea of white golfers. Our attention naturally gravitates to him.

Adherence to the Eight Laws

1. **The Law of Specialization.** He came into the professional game riding the reputation as the world's best amateur player, so he was known—and feared—before he ever lined up his first pro shot.

2. **The Law of Leadership.** You can't beat being regarded as the best in the world at something, and there are few people who don't think Woods is the best golfer alive.

3. **The Law of Personality.** His enthusiasm, his energy, his charisma and well-spoken nature all appear to be intrinsic in his personality. There appears to be little about Woods that's contrived.

4. **The Law of Distinctiveness.** He sets himself apart by slaughtering the rest of the field in the world's toughest golf tournaments—how's that for distinction? Beyond his victories, he also sets himself apart with his race and the wonderful imagery of his nickname.

5. **The Law of Visibility.** Even though the Buick endorsement didn't make much sense for a wealthy young guy, Woods has done a decent job of keeping himself in the public eye. His stellar golf game has done most of the work, though.

6. **The Law of Unity.** Woods's talkative father, Earl, makes it difficult to know just what the private Tiger is like, so this is a hard category to grade. Given that he's an open young man determined to follow his own advice, I'll give him the benefit of the doubt.

7. **The Law of Persistence.** It took years and years of work to make Woods this good. The guy has been swinging a club since age two, for crying out loud. Talent must be sharpened, and Woods's will to win has honed his talent to a razor edge.

8. **The Law of Goodwill.** As a champion athlete as well as a minority symbol, Woods is the subject of enormous admiration from the black community, young people, and the sports media. The only people who don't like him are the golfers he regularly defeats.

Influence in its Domain

Tiger Woods turned golf from a bigoted country club sport for portly white men into a hip game for middle class men of color. He made it cool—something no amount of marketing could have ever done. Woods's skills have opened new markets for golf...and his influence has introduced a generation of urban youngsters to a new kind of game.

Personal Brand Maintenance

Keeping a new Personal Brand relevant, effective, and in tune with the culture of the domain.

It should be obvious by now that a great Personal Brand is like a finely-tuned luxury car. It may run clean and strong for years, but it won't run forever without proper maintenance. You can't simply throw a Personal Brand into a domain without any support. Sooner or later, it will cease to be relevant and break down.

Once you've built a brand and begun to spread its influence, the next part of the equation is *maintenance*. The strongest Personal Brands are fluid, like their domains, and constant vigilance is needed to ensure they remain focused, effective, and targeted on the source's goals.

Is the Personal Brand Working?

As part of the Master Schedule, I've recommended evaluation periods, where you sit back and take careful note of how the Personal Brand is functioning in its domain. Regular evaluations are like oil changes for a brand—even if the brand isn't showing signs of wear, they're a preventive measure. There are three basic criteria by which to evaluate the Personal Brand you create:

1. **Short-term results:** Is your brand effective? That's the bottom line, and you can gauge it by looking at how both your domain's behavior and your opportunities have changed since your Personal Brand's

launch. Even changes that don't appear positive at the outset can be signs the brand is having an effect: people talking about you, forming stronger opinions about your work, and so on. Track changes within the domain over a six-month period, focusing on how people act, your reputation, increased or new opportunities, and changes in income. The greater the difference between the current period and the previous one, the more your Personal Brand is picking up momentum.

2. **Brand awareness:** Do people know who you are and what you stand for? Here, you need to assess how pervasive the Personal Brand is in its domain—a particularly critical issue for marketing and public relations pros. With observation and networking you should be able to calculate a rough percentage that shows how much of the domain is aware of the brand. Focus on two issues: people knowing the source's name, and people knowing what the source does or stands for. The percentage should always be increasing.

3. **Reaching goals:** A Personal Brand is a vehicle for reaching goals. Look at the goals you've set for the brand and determine if you're advancing toward them, or have actually reached them. Example: One of your goals is to get on the board of a prominent museum. If you make the board, that's one goal reached. Goals can involve pay, position, recognition, or many other factors.

Be Aware and Evolve

What if you've done your evaluation and the news isn't good? Your Personal Brand seems to be having no effect—or worse, a negative effect. What can you do? The best fix is to prevent such a thing from ever happening in the first place—and the key to accomplishing that is to cultivate *awareness*.

Awareness is the barometer of a Personal Brand's effectiveness. Look at the greatest commercial Personal Brands—Oprah, Madonna, Michael Jordan—and you'll see a common factor: they're all closely in touch with the culture of their domain, allowing them to evolve as their domain evolves. They don't make wrenching changes, but they adjust: new clothes here, a well-managed personal revelation there.

Awareness shows you whether you're still on course, but steering is up to you. You should be constantly aware of the cultural tides of your domain—through networking, conversation, reading trades, and the media. Cultivating awareness should become part of the daily routine of anyone building a Personal Brand. Some tips on building and using awareness:

1. Take notes. Watch your domain and note important changes or trends in writing.

2. Take notice of people whose faces or names keep surfacing. They're probably driving some sort of cultural change.

3. Talk. More important, listen. At parties, networking events or lunches, let others spill their stories.

4. Look for parallels. If you're aware of a cultural shift, look for another domain in which the same type of shift has taken place, like the dot-com world. What happened?

Change with the Culture

Earlier, I made the case against frivolously changing a Personal Brand, and that's still true. However, as the root culture of a domain changes—for example, if a university system decides to focus more on research and publishing than on teaching skills—it becomes crucial to be able to flex with the changes, to evolve with them and work new wrinkles into your Personal Brand.

A good example is author Stephen King. The Maine writer made himself the world's best-selling novelist on the backs of creepy stories of vampires, haunted hotels and children able to start fires with their minds. But as the culture's taste for horror stories began to dry up, he began to shift his style to more personal, psychological novels like *Rose Madder* and *Bag of Bones*. His sales are still sky-high, but he's shifted his mission to suit not only his audience, but his changing tastes as a writer.

Jumping Domains

Which brings us to a danger zone: jumping domains. The massive upside of a great Personal Brand has its downside: linkage with work or a set of traits that's so strong, you can't escape it. It's typecasting, where huge television stars never get a movie role. Imagine Stephen King writing bodice-ripper romance novels and you get an idea of how firmly some Personal Brands are embedded in our minds.

The danger in radically changing a Personal Brand to escape typecasting within your domain is that you could end up jumping into another domain. Example: an entrepreneur who founded several dot-coms during the Internet gold rush decides as the market gets more demanding, he's going to go where the easier money is: leasing office space to new companies. To him it seems like a lateral jump, but he finds himself in the real estate world, where his Personal Brand as an Internet whiz-kid means nothing. Soon, he's fighting just to stay out of bankruptcy.

The trick here is to evolve a Personal Brand gradually while staying within your domain. Being on the fringes is fine, but beware of stepping into new territory. A simple test will tell you if you've strayed: look at the org chart of the corporation you work for (or the organization you're consulting for) and ask yourself, "Do I know the key players in my company or my industry? Do they know me?" If the answers are negative, you've probably strayed into an adjacent domain where you don't want to be.

Warning Signs of Failure

Unless you're aware and constantly in touch with your domain, you won't know your brand is in a nose dive until it craters. Look sharp, continually evaluate, and rely on these three warning signs:

1. **Someone emulates you:** Actually, it's not just that someone copies your position, attributes or style. It's that they do it *better*. If you've billed yourself as the edgy, controversial talk radio personality in your market and someone comes along and out-Howard Sterns you, you've either built a brand identity that's not you or you're promoting it poorly.

2. **Lack of awareness:** The fuel for every Personal Brand is people knowing who you are and what you do. If no one does, you're in trouble. That's why evaluating brand awareness is so important; if yours hasn't increased since you launched your Personal Brand, one of two possibilities is at work – your identity is not memorable enough or you've done a rotten job of publicizing it.

3. **Negative reaction:** Some negative reaction is fine; if some more clueless people in your domain don't get your brand, big deal. But dislike, distrust or a general feeling of unwillingness to work with you are different matters altogether; it means you have seriously misjudged the culture and values of your domain.

Fine-Tuning Step-by-Step

Now you know all the things that can go wrong with your Personal Brand. But I'm not going to leave you hanging. There are precise steps you can take to assess the areas of weakness in your Personal Brand and correct them before you run into major problems and have to start from scratch.

1. **Check its relevance:** Does the Personal Brand identity—the values, traits and ideals it represents—still resonate with the domain? During the dot-com boom, the sloppy, swaggering computer programmer was perfectly in touch with the culture. But after the NASDAQ free fall, the arrogant, mercenary geek gets buried. If your brand has lost some of its relevance, some quick research should get you back in touch with what the domain considers important. Then you can work those characteristics into your brand.

2. **Check its authenticity:** Does the Personal Brand reflect who you are, what you care about and how you want to be seen by others? A brand that's out of tune with your personality and personal life can seem a small price to pay, but maintaining an inauthentic persona will wear on you and make your work less pleasurable. Take a candid look at the person you are and the person your Personal Brand says you are. If the two don't fit, changes are in order.

3. **Check your goals:** Goals change with time, especially as you discover the price of reaching them, or the likely rewards. Look at your goals from time to time and make sure they haven't changed.

4. **Check your competition:** Are you being copied? This is one of the most common problems with creating a successful Personal Brand: less imaginative people will follow your blueprint. The risks: dilution of your brand identity and confusion. But if you catch the competition early enough, you can adjust and take your brand in a new

direction, thereby making the competition look behind the times. *Aggressive, proactive moves are always preferable.* Don't wait for the other guy. If you're going to make mistakes, make big ones.

5. **Adjust your leading attribute:** If you're getting negative reactions or no reaction at all to your brand, you're not striking an emotional chord. That calls for changes to your leading attribute. Think of it as a radio signal; if you're not reaching your audience in the right way, keep broadcasting but adjust the signal. Keep adjusting until you affect your audience on an emotional as well as intellectual level.

6. **Adjust your brand expression:** Maybe the brand identity is fine, but you're not reaching people the way you hoped. It could be a tactical problem. How are you communicating your Personal Brand's characteristics and values? Is your message clear? Look at what you say and how you say it. If the message is vague, make it bolder and more direct, and get away from any hint of clichéd language. If the message is fine, look at ways to reach people that don't dilute your identity: articles, networking, a Web site, etc.

Bottom line, preventive Personal Brand maintenance will prevent 95 percent of the major problems your brand will ever encounter. The other 5 percent are unpredictable, and you're at the mercy of fate. But if you're constantly monitoring your brand and your domain and ready to bob, weave and adjust, you'll probably weather anything that comes your way.

Personal Brand Profile

John F. Kennedy
American Royalty

No United States President in modern times has provoked the love or the controversy of JFK, our thirty-fifth Chief Executive. His mention evokes a host of unforgettable images: graceful Jackie with her impeccable taste, the handsome family boating off Hyannisport, Kennedy's bold pledge to put a man on the moon before the end of the 1960s, and of course the shocking 1963 assassination. No one has embodied the ideal of the United States President more than Kennedy: handsome, vital, decisive and charismatic. That he was a man overflowing with contradictions has done nothing to dim his light.

John F. Kennedy (1917-1963)

The man who would be JFK—and one of the century's most tragic figures—was born in Brookline, Massachusetts, the second of Joseph and Rose Kennedy's nine children. Kennedy's childhood was marked by travel, mixing with New England society, and attendance at a series of private elementary schools, including a year at Canterbury School in New Milford, Connecticut, and four years at Choate School in Wallingford, Connecticut.

Kennedy spent the summer of 1935 studying at the London School of Economics, then entered Princeton University, but was forced to leave during his freshman year because of an attack of jaundice. In the fall of 1936, he enrolled at Harvard University, finally graduating *cum laude*. His early work as a journalist for the Hearst newspapers took him to San Francisco to cover the conference that laid the groundwork for the United Nations, and this exposure to politics led him to become a Democratic Congressman in 1947.

How This Brand Was Built

Grandson of former Boston mayor "Honey Fitz" Fitzgerald, Kennedy led a life of privilege from his childhood, and seemed destined for greatness. Harvard was followed by a heroic showing during World War II, when Kennedy led the crew of his sunken PT boat to safety. He moved quickly up the political ranks, a new type of politician: young, charming, good-looking, with a beautiful wife, a sense of East Coast style, and a Pulitzer Prize in his pocket for his book *Profiles in Courage*. Kennedy soon became the darling of Hollywood and the media, and in 1960 became the youngest (and first Catholic) president.

Aside from the Kennedy aura (which has produced as much tragedy as it has success), JFK's Personal Brand also sprang from his bold, successful policies, including the space program and the formation of the Peace Corps. But perhaps nothing cemented his legacy like the Cuban Missile Crisis, in which he led a United States-Soviet staredown over missile installations in Cuba. Kennedy had established himself as a man with ice water in his veins.

Of course, JFK's brand longevity was assured with his assassination, which transformed him from president to martyr. Stories of infidelities (including a reputed relationship with Marilyn Monroe) and other scandals were wiped away with his untimely death.

Why This Brand Works

- **Martyrdom:** Quite simply, Kennedy died before any of his rumored peccadilloes could tarnish his image of wholesome, all-American goodness. As a leader who died before his time, his faults were washed away in a wave of nostalgia.

- **Visibility:** He spent three years as the most visible man on earth, and that visibility only enhanced the public's perception of the

"Camelot" lifestyle: yachting excursions to Martha's Vineyard, the worship of Jackie's fashion sense, images of high-level talks with his brother Robert Kennedy, and so on.

- **Idealism:** Kennedy was the symbol of the America we wanted to see—vivacious, daring, rakish, able to accomplish anything. He represented the possibilities for the Space Age, and our dominance over the Russians.

- **Performance:** Kennedy was an effective president in more areas than his infamous standoff with the Soviets over Cuba. His economic programs launched the country on its longest sustained expansion since World War II. He promoted social legislation, including a federal desegregation policy in schools and universities, along with civil rights reform.

Adherence to the Eight Laws

1. **The Law of Specialization.** By virtue of becoming president, Kennedy stood out. By being the youngest president and the first Roman Catholic, he broke new ground.

2. **The Law of Leadership.** One could argue that the president is automatically a leader. But many presidents have been laughed at behind their backs or openly defied. Kennedy was in control, and set in motion policies that changed the United States for the better.

3. **The Law of Personality.** As with all politicians, JFK's real personality was buried beneath layers of media hype, campaign promises and myth. He appeared almost flawless, which is a good indication that his Personal Brand lacked authenticity of personality.

4. **The Law of Distinctiveness.** Kennedy was unlike any president since Teddy Roosevelt: active, rugged, a lover of the outdoors, a man's man before he was a politician. That was a great part of his appeal.

5. **The Law of Visibility.** He was the perfect president for the television age. Boyish, charismatic and silver-tongued, with the picture of the perfect First Lady by his side. The nation couldn't have designed a better couple to sit in the spotlight.

6. **The Law of Unity.** It's difficult to say how unified his brand was, since the many stories about affairs and other misdeeds have never been confirmed. But since the speculation remains, it stands to reason that Kennedy's public persona and his behavior behind closed doors did not always jibe.

7. **The Law of Persistence.** Kennedy fought through serious wounds in the war, major back surgery, and the death of one of his children in infancy to win a tough 1960 campaign against Richard Nixon. Any man who successfully runs the presidential gauntlet deserves to be called a survivor.

8. **The Law of Goodwill.** In Massachusetts, he's one step down from a deity. In the rest of the nation, he's merely revered. JFK remains a symbol of the 1960s spirit that led us to the moon, and is still regarded by many as one of our greatest presidents.

Influence in its Domain

Rather than having much direct effect on politics, the Personal Brand of John Kennedy influences us as a model of what a president *can* be. However, with his assassination seen by many people as the grim harbinger of the modern media age and modern political violence, he continues to influence our entire culture.

CHAPTER SIXTEEN

Personal Brand Power Rankings

Who are the twenty-five greatest of our time?

Who has the most powerful Personal Brand of all time? To be sure, it's a subjective question. Some brands hold tremendous resonance for some people but have little around the globe. But for our purposes, the question is simple: What twenty-five Personal Brands retain the most power to influence the way we think, act, feel and spend our money?

I approached this daunting task with a few important criteria in mind:

1. The people could be dead or alive

2. They could be from any period in history

3. The people should be global, not just examples of American culture

4. They had to be real people, not creations such as Ronald McDonald

How to rank such people? It's an inexact science at best, but I decided to rank the candidate brands by the following five criteria:

1. **Icon Status:** Does the person represent a concept larger than himself or herself? If so, how clear is that representation, and does anyone else share it?

2. **Reach:** How large is the Personal Brand's domain, and how well-known is the person within that domain?

3. **Influence:** Within his or her domain, how much influence does the Personal Brand wield?

4. **Revenue:** How much revenue was the Personal Brand responsible for, directly or indirectly, in the last calendar year?

5. **Goodwill:** What is the level of goodwill toward the Personal Brand? Remember that goodwill is the difference between a *great* and a *powerful* Personal Brand.

This is hardly a definitive analysis, and there are sure to be people who disagree completely. After all, the power of a Personal Brand is very subjective, and different brands have power in different parts of the world. But based on my expertise and that of my research team, I feel this is a strong, representative ranking of the twenty-five greatest Personal Brands of all time, to date.

2001 Personal Brand Power Rankings

1. Jesus Christ
2. Michael Jordan
3. Mohandas K. Gandhi
4. Walt Disney
5. Oprah Winfrey
6. Mother Teresa
7. Albert Einstein
8. Muhammad Ali
9. Tiger Woods
10. Larry King
11. Martin Luther King, Jr.
12. Abraham Lincoln
13. Bill Gates
14. William Shakespeare
15. Elvis Presley
16. John Lennon
17. Jack Welch
18. Tom Cruise
19. Stephen King
20. Madonna
21. Charles Schwab
22. Stephen Spielberg
23. Frank Sinatra
24. Martha Stewart
25. Jackie Robinson

*You may wildly disagree with our choices of the Greatest Personal Brands. Great. Visit www.petermontoya.com and vote in our annual "Greatest Personal Brands" survey. In the future, we'll use only reader input to calculate these brand rankings.

Personal Brand Profile

Jesus Christ
Savior

It may seem crass and reductive to talk about Jesus Christ in the context of a Personal Brand. After all, Jesus began his ministry with no desire for self-promotion; he ministered to offer mankind salvation. The apostles and disciples credited as the authors of the New Testament intended first and foremost to share the Good News, not to promote a "brand."

However, there's no getting around it: the purity of Christ's personal mission led directly to the pervasiveness of the religion founded in his name. In that sense, Jesus of Nazareth is the single most influential Personal Brand of the last 2000 years. Jesus did not set out to create a Personal Brand, but today, his Personal Brand is more influential than any other. This is because, Mohammed and Buddha notwithstanding, Jesus Christ is arguably the most influential person who ever lived. Billions of people base their daily actions, their morality, their beliefs, their purpose and even their reproductive choices on his teachings. Jesus' Personal Brand continues to grow—and grow—fueled by the public's belief not only in his Gospel, but in his personal righteousness.

When you examine Jesus Christ through the definition of a Personal Brand—the power to influence the emotions, perceptions and actions of others—Jesus' brand is as big as it gets.

Jesus Christ [6-5 B.C.-30-33 A.D.]

Myth and religious tradition blur fact in the biography of Jesus, but scholars believe he was born in Bethlehem, sometime before the death of Herod the Great in 4 B.C. He grew to manhood and learned the trade of a carpenter at the hands of his father, Joseph, and mother, Mary. His ministry, however, began in Nazareth.

After being baptized by John the Baptist in the river Jordan, Jesus gathered a group of twelve close followers or apostles, the number perhaps being symbolic of the twelve tribes of Israel and indicative of an aim to reform the Jewish religion of his day. Records as well as the New Testament gospels depict conflicts with the Pharisees over his exercise of an independent "prophetic" authority, but his arrest by the Jewish spiritual hierarchy appears to have resulted more directly from his action against the Temple in Jerusalem.

The duration of Jesus' public ministry is uncertain, but John's Gospel suggests a three-year period of teaching. Jesus was executed by crucifixion under the order of Pontius Pilate, the Roman procurator, perhaps because of the unrest his activities were causing.

How This Brand Was Built

The first step was Jesus' ministry. The second step occurred during A.D. 55-95, when the books of the New Testament were written by the apostles—Paul, James, Peter, John, Mark, Matthew, and others who actually knew Jesus of Nazareth.

With the dissemination of the Gospels, the Good News spread far and wide. And within 100 years, the Roman Catholic Church appeared as a point of coalition for the early Christians. The church would become a world power with the rise of the Popes and the fall of polytheistic Rome, and it represented the administrative support network essential to the worldwide growth of Christ's Personal Brand.

From the Middle Ages to the twenty-first century, that growth has been steady. Even the dawn of science and Darwin haven't shaken the foundations of Christianity—a religious amplification not only of Jesus' ministry, but also of his Personal Brand. His Personal

Brand has inspired belief and action for nearly twenty centuries. That's extraordinary.

Why This Brand Works

- **Authority:** Talk about credibility and authority. Most Christians view the Gospel as the absolute, infallible rulebook on human behavior, and as the source of knowledge of God's kingdom. More moderate, mainline Christians also live their lives devoutly by its principles—principles first expressed by one man.

- **Reflection of Value:** Few other Personal Brands have had values grafted onto them like the Personal Brand of Jesus: layers of religious dissonance, propaganda and cultural baggage have obscured aspects of his message to the point where wildly divergent actions are claimed to be justified by the Gospel. People have compassionately helped the poor in the name of the Lord; people have bombed abortion clinics in his name.

- **Emotional Power:** Issues like sin, salvation, eternal life and damnation invoke volatile, overwhelming emotions that can shake communities, change the course of nations and alter entire cultures. Think about the Crusades. Few people have neutral feelings about the man from Galilee.

- **Timelessness:** Jesus can't be discredited, degraded, or misquoted. The New Testament portrays him as a sinless man; if he had any "human" flaws, they have been erased by time and his ascension to the throne of the world's most powerful religion. He has millions of missionaries doing work in his name the world over, a collective church infrastructure to support Christianity, and adherents who will believe in his unquestionable divinity. His Personal Brand is immortal.

Adherence to the Eight Laws

1. **The Law of Specialization.** If you're a Christian, there's only one Savior. You can't get any more specialized than this.

2. **The Law of Leadership.** When you're omnipotent, omniscient, and eternal, it's hard not to be the leader in your field.

3. **The Law of Personality.** Jesus' human personality has become lost in time, and when it's suggested that he had flaws and weaknesses like the rest of us, such as in Martin Scorsese's *Last Temptation of Christ*, the result is protest. The divine Jesus has an eternal aura of benevolence and love, rather than a human personality.

4. **The Law of Distinctiveness.** Again, it helps to be the only savior in your faith. Jesus—and no one else—equals eternal life for the Christian.

5. **The Law of Visibility.** Billions of people pray to him, talk about him, build churches to worship him, hold concerts praising him, and so on. His Personal Brand is still the world's most visible.

6. **The Law of Unity.** In word and deed, Jesus lived the ultimate life of unity.

7. **The Law of Persistence.** Jesus was so persistent in living a life consistent with his beliefs that he was crucified.

8. **The Law of Goodwill.** The overwhelming perception of Jesus is of a kindly, wise, just, forgiving figure who will love us no matter how badly we sin.

Influence in its Domain

Jesus Christ's domain—Christianity—is, in fact, his Personal Brand. The effects of that Personal Brand can be felt at every level of Western society. It motivates charitable giving, comforts the bereaved, breeds the occasional cult, and, at the most mundane level, fuels a Christmas economy. The Personal Brand of Jesus Christ profoundly affects nearly every aspect of human life, and lives around the world. Its might is without peer.

The Twenty-First Century Brand

Can a person and Personal Brand coexist in the new millennium?

We've come a long way from the random perceptions of others to the sophistication and subtlety of the Personal Brand. You now know that the Personal Brand is the currency for success in the coming century. Hopefully, you've acquired some of the tools to understand, leverage and benefit from Personal Branding, or at least the knowledge to know it's not for you. Because while you can use it, reject it or fight it, one thing you can't do is ignore it.

So, a few final issues:

Can a Personal Brand still be a person?

Yes. In fact, it's crucial. People like Howard Stern, who disappear into their brands, usually end up unhappy where it counts—in their personal lives. There's no reason having a strong Personal Brand should be dehumanizing; quite the opposite, in fact. The process of creating a Personal Brand can make you more aware of your most valuable qualities, and bring your key values into clearer focus.

Should a Personal Brand last a lifetime?

It can. The greatest brands, those founded on public service and a mission to promote the greater good, remain strong long after their sources have died. William Shakespeare, Mozart and Abraham Lincoln are examples of colossal Personal Brands that have only grown in fascination and resonance for us, long after the people have become dust.

You'll find a Personal Brand develops organically, over time. As its creator, you're like a surfer riding a long, challenging wave: how far you ride depends on your skill, but you can't control how the wave is going to break. You've got to be prepared to ride with the changes. Waves never stay still, and neither do brands.

The Power of Perception Management

Personal Branding is perception management. It's about taking as much risk and chance as possible out of the complex dynamic of human interaction and perception—all to help you obtain better opportunities and build a better life.

Personal Branding doesn't harm anyone, doesn't brainwash, and doesn't treat people like they're stupid. What it does is respect the intelligence of the audience by assuming that if you can't perform as advertised, and your brand is based on falsehood, your audience will be sharp enough to figure it out and send you packing.

Personal Branding maneuvers to allow the best and smartest to rise to the top, and the most skilled to be the most appreciated. It's the ultimate system of merit: if you put yourself out there, you'd better be able to do what you say you can do.

Personal Branding and the Internet

The genie is out of the bottle. The Internet has changed Personal Branding in countless ways: made communication instant and multi-point, allowed anyone and everyone to create their own marketing presence and their own band of followers, nurtured a culture of anonymously spread rumor and complaint, and much more.

When it comes to your Personal Brand, the Internet is both a blessing and curse. It allows you to communicate with a vast array of people within a domain in seconds; it also allows those people to circulate negative reviews of your work in just as little time. Follow the same process with the Internet that you do with any other part of the Personal Branding arena: understand it, manage it, leverage it.

That means understanding how e-mail works, above all. E-mail, not the Web, is the "killer app" of the Internet. Learn about newsgroups, posting boards and the like. Carry out a "preemptive strike" of information by launching your own Web site and your own online discussion group; such steps will preemptively counter negative information over which you have no control.

Most important, use the Internet to be better at whatever you do. Speed up communication, improve research, manage teams—be a better professional.

Beware Your Press Clippings

Popular culture is bursting with iconic Personal Brands who got too caught up in their images, believed the stories about themselves, felt pressure to live up to those perceptions, and ended up falling hard. Jim Morrison, John Belushi, Princess Diana—there's almost no high-profile tragic death of the last forty years that doesn't reflect some aspect of the individual becoming a prisoner of his or her public persona.

Do not believe your press clippings—what others say about you, what may be written about you, what your marketing or promotional materials say. A person and a Personal Brand are not one and the same, and anyone who forgets this is asking for trouble. Believing bad press can lead to depression and a loss of mission, while swallowing good press or your own image-making often leads to arrogance, complacency and alienation of the audience you worked so hard to capture. Never lose sight of the fact that your Personal Brand is packaging. Keep refining it, but avoid being replaced by it.

To Thine Own Self Be True

Finally, a little quote from Act I, Scene III of *Hamlet*, courtesy of the aforementioned Mr. Shakespeare:

> *"This above all, to thine own self be true.*
> *And it must follow, as the night the day,*
> *Thou canst not then be false to any man."*

Therein lies the heart of the great Personal Brand: let your brand reflect who you really are. If there's a sin in this marketing-blinded age, it's falsehood or hypocrisy, practiced by a man who claims to be one thing while being another, thumbing his nose at a public too stupid to figure him out. News flash: the public always figures it out.

Being true to yourself in your Personal Brand results in an identity that reflects your true strengths, connects with others because it does not hide your flaws, has unity because there's nothing to hide, and is supportable because the values and talents behind the brand are your values and talents.

In the end, the great Personal Brand isn't about research and target audiences and awareness, but about the person behind the brand. Ignore advice to be slicker, more saleable, or more like someone else. Be unique and damn the trends. You might end up creating one.

Index

H

I

J

Glossary

Attribute: A distinctive, compelling characteristic that communicates an intellectual or emotional benefit to a Personal Brand's domain. Most Personal Brands have 3-6 attributes.

Audience: Everyone exposed to the Personal Brand, targeted or not.

Brand Equity: Having "ownership" of a portion of a domain's perceptions by driving home a Personal Brand message until that message is part of the domain's culture.

Characteristic: Any basic human trait, from eye color and accent to sense of humor and eating habits.

Domain: The sphere of influence—a group of individuals, a company, multiple related companies or an entire industry—in which your Personal Brand is established.

Entrepreneur: Those who work for themselves: attorneys, chiropractors, consultants, CPAs, dentists, physicians, writers, designers, photographers, financial advisors, mortgage brokers, stockbrokers, real estate professionals, speakers, trainers.

Leading Attribute: The single most potent attribute, the one thing the Personal Brand will be known for above all others. (Ex: Michael Jordan's leading attribute is "Greatest basketball player of all time.")

Personal Brand: A personal identity that stimulates precise, meaningful perceptions in its audience about the values and qualities the person stands for.

Personal Branding: The process of creating a Personal Brand by 1) determining your ideal professional identity (who you are); 2) which of your abilities carry the greatest potential value (what you do); and 3) how you can benefit your domain.

Personal Identity: The name or description most often used to identify you—your name, your profession, a description of how you do your work. (Ex: "He's that temperamental photographer.")

Personal Image: The superficial surface elements of a person. They can include physical appearance, apparel, ethnic background and speaking style.

Personal Marketing: Using your Personal Brand in the pursuit of business development.

Position: A statement that defines the niche you occupy in your chosen field, and the "space" you occupy in the perceptions of your target audience.

Professional: A skilled individual who works for someone else in a corporate or small business environment.

Proxy Self: A brand "presence" that is known to the people in a domain, and influences their behavior and decisions on the source's behalf even when the source is not present.

Response Cue: Individual bits of information, often expressed through marketing or identity materials, designed to evoke an emotional response in a Personal Brand's domain.

Slogan: A statement that explains what you do, who you do it for and/or the benefit.

Source: The human being behind the Personal Brand—the originator of the carefully packaged, projected persona that's the public face for the person beneath.

Target Audience: The individuals or organizations within your domain to whom you will promote your Personal Brand. The subset of your domain that offers you the greatest advancement and income potential while having the greatest need for the benefit you offer.

Peter Montoya: From Personal Branding to Personal Triumph

This isn't the typical author biography, but this isn't your typical book. In the definitive guide to Personal Branding, it seemed right to use one of the most powerful Personal Marketing tools, the Personal Brochure, to tell you a little about myself. So off we go.

>>>

Start With Good People

Many times I've been asked the secret of a strong company, and I always give the same answer: "Great people." Of course, I was lucky enough to learn about people in the best way imaginable: growing up in a big, crazy Southern California family.

There were a few jokes about the biblical names of us five boys—John, Matthew, Mark, Luke and Peter—but mostly there was fun, laughter and love. In this time I learned an important lesson: it's not talent or education that determine a person's value, but integrity, compassion and hard work. As I got older, I knew I wanted to associate with those kinds of people.

An after-hours creative session with some of the team.

A Journey of Enlightenment

Fascinated with the concepts of personal image and individual marketing, I was determined to absorb it all. I spent two-and-a-half years working for the country's largest sales and personal development trainer. Here I discovered that while step-by-step instruction is the key to success, a turnkey approach doesn't work; every pupil has different needs.

My next stop, a personal marketing firm, was an inspiration more for what they were missing than for what they were doing. Here I began to understand and develop the core principles of Personal Branding, as well as its organic nature. My next move would be my own.

Me and two of my best friends—Maxine and Molly dressed up for Halloween.

A Risk Worth Taking

Founding Peter Montoya, Inc. in 1997 was the boldest move I had ever made—and the riskiest. In the early days, when I was broke, I sold my house to keep the company afloat.

But I never doubted what I was doing. I've always believed that Personal Branding was a fundamental business force just waiting to be understood. I was determined to be the one who revealed its power to the world.

That mission has led me to innovate—launching the magazine *Peter Montoya's Personal Branding* and creating my unique "What's Your Brand?" seminar, for example. But the success I've had so far—including this book—has ultimately been the result of exhaustive work fueled by an absolute dedication to an idea I passionately believe in.

Me with some of my family: Mom (Denise), John, Matt, Mark and Luke.

Full Circle

Today, I've come back to family, by creating two families of my own. First, on New Year's Eve 2001, I married Lynn, the love of my life and my true inspiration. Second, I'm fortunate enough to have populated Peter Montoya, Inc. with some of the most extraordinary

The love of my life and I at our big night, December 31, 2001.

people I've ever had the privilege to know. They're my family, too.

So it really does come down to people. Find good ones who match your dedication and turn them loose. Stay true to the mission and your passion, and don't be afraid to risk something new.

It's sure worked for me.

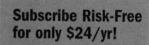

The biggest Personal Brands...
in their own words.

Personal Brandstorming with Peter Montoya Audio CD

There's nothing like hearing information straight from the source, and that's what you get with *Personal Brandstorming*. On this audio CD, you'll listen to a candid conversation between Peter Montoya and some of today's most influential Personal Brands—entrepreneurs, athletes, entertainers and politicians.

They'll reveal:

> How they built their brand
> What they've done to sustain it
> How they turned it into a strategic tool

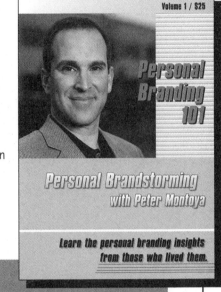

Volume 1 / $25

Personal Branding 101

Personal Brandstorming with Peter Montoya

Learn the personal branding insights from those who lived them.

Get Personal Brandstorming with Peter Montoya for only $25! (866) 288-9300 or www.petermontoya.com

In your car, at your office or relaxing at home, sit back and learn firsthand how today's best Personal Brands got where they are—and how their experiences can help you build your brand!

Order *Personal Brandstorming with Peter Montoya #1* for only $25!

Call *(866) 288-9300* or go to *www.petermontoya.com* today to order, and discover the Personal Branding secrets of the people who are making it work.

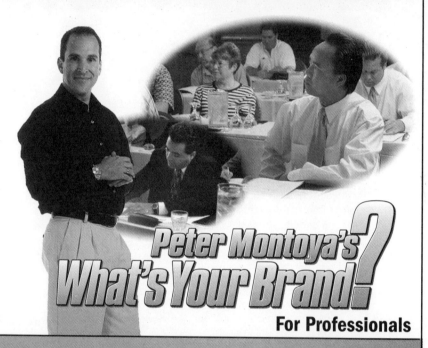

Peter Montoya's
The Brand Called You
For Entrepreneurs
Register today: (866) 288-9300 or www.petermontoya.com

Here's What You'll Learn...

Personal Brochures

My writers and designers have created hundreds of stunning Personal Brochures for clients of all types—conservative, wild, urban, rural, you name it—in every industry. Use our knowledge to create the most important Personal Branding tool you'll ever have.

Personal Postcards

Personal Branding demands continual communication, and direct mail makes it happen. Learn what top branding strategists do to develop a direct response schedule—a schedule that can work with your market, and within your budget.

Brand Identity:
Logos & Stationery

"Identity" means logo, slogan, business cards and letterhead. These elements are often a prospect's first point of contact, so they need to be impressive and professional. Your personality and style must be encapsulated in a logo that reflects who you are and instantly communicates to your audience what makes you unique.

GWENDOLY

K

**KIRKLAND
BROWN CFP**

An architect to design
your financial future.

Web Sites

A Web site is no longer optional; it's essential. You'll learn how to design a site that's not about fancy graphics, but about meeting your strategic goals. Whether you need online applications and functionality or a powerful lead-gathering tool, you'll learn how to use the Internet as a resource that works.

Custom One-Year Marketing & Branding Plans

How do you get your brand message out? What tactics do you use? What are your goals? Every Personal Brand begins with these questions—and we'll show you the answers.

Register today: (866) 288-9300 or www.petermontoya.com

At The Brand Called You,® you'll learn the branding techniques of billion-dollar Personal Brands.

> How to control your client's perception of you by creating and instilling your position.

> How to select a precise target market that will earn you far more money than marketing to everyone.

> How to tap into the incredible power of marketing channels, including networking and professional referrals.

> Direct mail mistakes to avoid, and how to use direct mail correctly to attract clients and generate referrals.

> How to name your practice, and create a slogan to help your Personal Brand grow into a market-moving force.

> Master the Web site secrets that will transform your portal into a client-servicing, business-generating power-port.

Sign up today!

For pricing, locations and upcoming dates call **(866) 288-9300** or go to **www.petermontoya.com**.

PeterMontoya Inc.
The Leaders in Personal Branding

Register today: (866) 288-9300 or www.petermontoya.com